memoir

L

Growing up in Byron Bay during the 60s and 70s, Richard (Ric) Light took to surfing and sport but, despite his father being the English Master, had little interest in school. After stumbling through his first few post-school years and attending Lismore Teachers College, he embarked on a teaching career first at primary school, and then at secondary school in Australia. He then taught at secondary school level in Japan before returning to Australia to complete a PhD in Human Movement at The University of Queensland.

Richard's academic career saw him promoted to professor eight years later and becoming a leading international thinker and researcher in the development of innovative sport coaching and physical education teaching. His twenty-year career included appointments in Australia, the UK and New Zealand, and positions as invited professor in highly regarded universities in Japan, Canada, and France. In 2021, he returned to his hometown of Byron Bay as Professor Emeritus at the University of Canterbury in New Zealand and flies down to The University of Sydney to teach casually during semester. Over his career, he has published more than 200 journal articles and book chapters, and 12 academic books on sport and physical education, but *Grief and Growth* is his first non-academic book. He had a story he had to tell and one he thought that many readers could relate to and learn from. It is a story about dealing with the loss of loved ones, and how it promoted personal, professional, and spiritual growth that gave life deep meaning.

The Digital Publishing Centre @ IP
Interactive Publications Pty Ltd
Brisbane

Photo: Sam Canning

Grief and Growth

Professor Richard Light

Digital Publishing Centre @ IP
an imprint of IP (Interactive Publications Pty Ltd)
Treetop Studio • 9 Kuhler Court
Carindale, Queensland, Australia 4152
sales@ipoz.biz
http://ipoz.biz/shop
First published by IP in 2024
© 2024, IP and Richard Light

Printed in 16 pt Avenir Book on Caslon Pro 12 pt.

ISBN: 9781922830579 (PB) 9781922830586 (eBook)

A catalogue record for this book is available from the National Library of Australia

To my wife Chiho for her tolerance and support of my unwavering commitment to getting this book published and to my daughter Amy as a way of sharing my life and values with her.

Acknowledgements

Book design: David P. Reiter
Author photo: Sam Canning

I would like to acknowledge the assistance of the following people who offered feedback on drafts of the book or specific chapters and/or checked dates, names and place names for authenticity:

Amy Light, Melbourne; Andrew Hilton, Mount Tamborine, Qld; Bill Connor, Byron Bay; Brian Mahoney, Osaka, Japan; David Eckford, Osaka, Japan; Eric Walker, Ballina; Jenny Clarke, Christchurch, New Zealand; John Fysh, Byron Bay; Simon Greaves, Byron Bay, Vanessa Wells, Bilgola Plateau, Sydney.

Contents

My Early Years in the Bay

My brother Greg and I let gravity carry us down the track until we hit the beach and the sand squeaked under our feet as we bolted toward The Pass. Standing in the strong summer sun, I watched the small, smooth waves peeling off as they passed by with my younger brother beside me, and not another human in sight. Lost in the rhythm and sounds of the ocean, the immortal reach of the sky, the enormity of nature, I felt small and insignificant. My introduction to Byron Bay was powerful and moving as we both stood in silence, and in awe of the nature that surrounded us.

"Wow. I've never seen anything like this" Greg said to me.

"Me either. It's so big." I replied, looking out over the expansive ocean.

Without much more said, we walked back to Clarkes beach, picking up shells and pieces of driftwood that had washed up on the beach, regularly stopping to look around and take in where we were. After walking back up the sandy track we had earlier charged down, we crossed the road and walked back into reality. We were both keen to have a surf but had to help move into our new home and set up the bedroom we would share. With a father who surfed, I knew we'd get a chance soon but also knew that we had work to do. I tried to focus on the jobs he gave me but was easily distracted by views of the ocean from the house. I had always struggled to apply myself to anything that did not interest me and couldn't help thinking about the magic of our brief experience at The Pass. Glimpses of the glistening ocean and the beautiful lines of swells that had wrapped around the cape made it difficult to focus on the tasks our parents gave us.

I started surfing at North Avalon in Sydney four years before arriving in Byron Bay, but it was limited to only one or two surfs on the weekend, if conditions were good and we didn't live anywhere near the beach from my first day living in Lighthouse Road, it was very different. I felt connected with the ocean and had a feeling I was where I belonged. Despite us all being tired from the long drive up from Sydney, conversation at the dinner table on the first night was lively and focused on the amazing new environment or family now lived in.

"Well, what do you all think of Byron Bay?" asked our father with a hint of satisfaction,

"It's great. I can't believe the beach and can't wait to have a surf" I replied,

"Yeah, we walked all the way to the end of the beach to those big rocks. The ocean is really big, and the surf looks good. If we can have a surf that would be great. Can I get a proper surfboard for coming to Byron Bay?" Greg asked,

"Certainly Greg. Just give me time to settle in and get some things done then we'll look for a board you can ride. There's a surf shop in town called San Juan. We can drop in there to see if they have any second-hand boards."

The mood at the table was very positive with all of us happy about moving to Byron Bay, and into our wonderful new home. When our father Bill told Greg and me that we were leaving Sydney to live in Byron Bay we were horrified. It was our world with our networks of friends that I felt he wanted to rip us away from. We knew nothing about Byron Bay and complained all the way up from Sydney in the old lime green holden station wagon from Bilgola Plateau. That was until we crested St Helena to be confronted by the stunning view of Byron Bay and the ocean, stretching out as far as we could see. I had never had such a feeling of how big the world was and being on top of it.

"Is that Byron Bay?" I asked after a few seconds' silence in the car.

"Yes, it is, Ric" he replied with satisfaction.

"Wow. That's where we are going to live?" Greg asked.

Our mother Betty looked so happy at the dinner table on that first night and, as always, waited in the background listening to what was being said before saying anything. herself. Our father led the conversation and was clearly very pleased with the beginning of a new life for our family that he had set up, and his promotion to English Master at Mullumbimby High School. I suspect he was also relieved at how quickly Greg, and I stopped complaining and took to our new home. Only six years old and missing a few teeth, Sue seemed a little confused. She asked what the school she would attend at the end of the Christmas holidays was like, what the teachers were like and what she would do. Our parents painted a very positive picture for her and then she asked:

"Can I get a horse mummy?"

"Well…. maybe but let's wait until you go to school then think about it? "

"We'd have to find a paddock somewhere to keep it and you'd have to look after it" our father added."

"Yes, I'll look after it. I want a shiny black horse and I want to ride it along the beach."

Our father was busy but found time to take Greg and me for a surf the next day with the waves small, a light offshore wind from the south and only another four or five surfers out at The Pass. He took us again for a short surf the next day when I recognised a few boys my age in the water from the day before. It looked like they were good mates, yelling encouragement to each other and calling to claim waves or to give them to their mates as each new set approached. Envious of their little group and the fun they seemed to be having, I caught the eye of a couple of them waiting for a set (of waves). We exchanged perfunctory nods of recognition, but nothing was said. Listening to their conversations, it was obvious they were local boys who went to the school I was enrolled in.

The next day Greg and I went for a morning surf on our own and as we got to the top of the hill overlooking the beach, we could see that the swell had picked up a little with four-foot waves peeling off from The Pass and down to Clarkes beach. Not knowing the banks or the ins and outs of surfing at our new home beach, we were a little apprehensive. Walking along the beach to The Pass, I felt excited but anxious when we saw that nobody was out surfing. We didn't want to turn back so sat down in the sand at The Pass, watching beautiful, unridden waves peeling off. We wanted to go out but were worried about being on our own and could feel the power of nature all around us. At only nine years old and riding a Coolite board, Greg did not want to go out, and I didn't want to go out on my own.

"Hey, look!" Greg said with excitement when he saw two surfers who looked about the same ages as us, walking along the beach toward us. As they approached us, we both stood up.

"Waves look pretty good. Are you going out?" said the boy about my age.

I nodded. "We were just having a look at how the waves are breaking before we go out. We've only surfed here a couple of times."

"I'm Barry and this is Brett. Where are you guys from?"

"Bilgola Plateau. In Sydney. We just moved up here a few days ago. I'm Ric and this is my little brother, Greg."

"Oh, yeah, just up there in the white house. In Lighthouse Road" he said pointing toward where our home was.

"Yeah. Just arrived and getting used to it. Surf looks great here. Are you guys going out now?

"Yeah, we are. Let's go out together. I'll show you where to paddle out."

I couldn't wait to catch my first wave and loved my introduction to surfing in Byron Bay. We were soon joined by a few other locals and with long breaks between sets, conversation led to learning about other local surf breaks, the local surf shop, and the high school that I would attend in a few weeks. I was stunned to find out I would go to school on a train and felt most comfortable with Mick who became one of my best mates in the Bay. Seemed to me that all these local guys did was surf, and in the best surf I had ever seen. They also told me about how they sometimes rocked the occasional corrugated iron roof on a Friday or Saturday night and other thrills when there was no surf, and they were bored. Over the two hours I was surfing I learned so much about the town, the school, and the lifestyle I was looking forward to experiencing. Just before I caught my last wave, I met one of my next-door neighbours, Eric.

After little more than a week, it seemed like Greg and I were becoming part of the local group of young surfers which was confirmed when invited to join a few of them for a surf at Tallow (Beach). A strong northerly had blown out the surf on the north facing beaches and three or four of them were going to walk to Tallow because it is protected by Cape Byron from the north easterly wind. A handful of us agreed to make an early start and prepare for what could be a long day if the surf was good. I took a small backpack with a large bottle of water, an apple, a couple of peanut butter sandwiches for Greg and me, some sun cream and wax. I wore a T-shirt, my board shorts, and thongs.

We met at the turnoff from Lighthouse Road early in the morning and headed off. Full of cheer and chatter, we started walking toward Tallow where we expected the waves in Cosy Corner would be very good. We had long heavy boards to carry but were in a good mood because we knew that at the end of the long walk we would be riding powerful, smooth waves with very few other surfers. Standing on the sand dunes, the waves in Cosy Corner looked great so picked up our pace on the last leg of our little journey. From the dunes to Cosy Corner, we walked as quickly as we could, with bursts of excited conversation when we saw hard breaking left handers thumping the bank in shallow water.

At Cosy Corner, we surfed for four or five hours with lots of talking between sets, and on the beach during breaks for water and snacks. The conversations varied from talking about surfing to school and girls. Mick was popular with the girls and a smooth talker who told me about a few of them at school that he wanted me to meet. He said they'd like me and that he'd set me up with a couple of them when we started the new school year. Everything was happening so fast for me that I felt like I was in a dream and the natural environment all around me blew me out.

By midday, the surf was deteriorating as the northerly became stronger and blew in more from the east, we were all tired, and there was no food or water left so we headed home. As we trudged along a dry and dusty dirt road under the hot summer sun, my board grew heavier with each step, conversation ran out, and I started to feel hungry. Over the last two hundred metres Greg and I could think and talk about nothing but what we would eat when we got home, and the pace picked up. From the time we entered our front yard the race was on. We dropped our boards on the grass and bolted up the steps, jostling shoulder to shoulder. I got an early start and managed to get through the front door before Greg for the sprint to the kitchen bench where we gorged on bread and peanut butter. Mum sat calmly at the dining table watching the feeding frenzy of her lively, energetic sons, full of pride.

Greg got his first real surfboard and was initially intimidated by the powerful waves at The Pass when the swell was up but within a year, was taking on the challenging bank in front of Spectators and surfing four foot waves from The Pass to Clarkes beach then carrying his board back. I loved surfing in Byron Bay and not only because of the waves. The connection with the ocean, the big seabirds, often flying close to the water, and pods of dolphins that sometimes surfed the same wave I was on placed me deep in nature. What I saw, heard and felt when waiting for waves made surfing a magical experience, but it was also scary at times.

Riding four-to-five-foot waves at The Pass, smoothed by a gentle southerly during my second year in the Bay, I was lost in the flow of catching and riding waves, then paddling back out. Waiting for the next set, something caught my eye, and I looked down to see a massive dark shape slowly and menacingly passing below me. The sudden shift from pleasure to fear rattled me and I pulled my feet up as quickly as I could without betraying my fear. I then paddled in, but not before speaking to a couple of nearby surfers:

"Did you see that big Noah just now?"

"Mate, I'll take my chances," one said. "Too good not to go in."

"It's not interested in us, mate" said the other, suddenly paddling off to catch a wave.

The glimpse of that huge shark only metres below their dangling legs did not seem to worry too many of them.

My next close encounter with a big shark was two years later when surfing with Greg at Broken Head, late in the day with the sun sinking in the west. All the other surfers had gone in as we sat on our boards, waiting for our last wave, with the sun setting. Straining to see the next set of waves approach, a huge shark's dorsal fin broke the surface of the water only ten metres from us. We both froze.

"Fuck," was all I could say.

"Let's go!" was Greg's reply. We quickly yet, as quietly as possible, paddled in while trying not to panic. It was massive, and I was relieved to feel the sand under my feet on the beach.

I had several encounters with sharks when snorkelling or spear fishing as well as surfing. Among them was the odd experience of running into a pack of young tiger sharks swimming in two lines at the wreck (the *Tassie 3*) in front if the swimming pool when spearfishing with my father. From the surface, I could see what I thought were big fish approaching so took a breath to dive down with my spear gun to see what they were. Taking a vertical dive to get down deep, I did not see what they were until I was close to them. I was stunned and froze but they ignored me and passed by me. I returned to the surface and swam into shore. After decades of feeding on whale meat and then offal pumped into the ocean from the abattoirs, sharks saw the jetty as a favourite haunt. They always worried me, but other locals did not share my fear. Before it was demolished in 1972, a couple of the more-crazy locals would jump from the 'new' jetty to divebomb smaller sharks for a thrill. The startled shark would take off in fright while the crazy local would clamber up one of the pylons and back up onto the jetty to the cheers and laughter of his mates.

Surfing was the main source of thrills for me and my mates, but, when there were no waves, the powerful natural environment of the Bay offered alternatives. Sometimes we would walk around to Little Beach then clamber over jagged rocks to the rage hole. When there was a good swell, waves smashed violently against the wall of rock between the narrow gutter of the rage hole and the ocean with thick white plumes of spray exploding skyward. Waves surged powerfully into the long gutter to push up and over the flat rocks around it and as each surge retreated, the water was sucked back into the gutter over a ledge to form a hard sheet of powerfully flowing water.

High on adrenaline, I'd wait for the next wave to push up the gutter before jumping into the churning water with Greg to be carried up and over the rock ledge. As the water rushed back over the ledge, I had to stay calm, focus, and go with the flow until I sensed where the ledge was to grab it with both hands. Suspended in the echoing space between the rock wall and the huge mass of water thundering over us, Greg and I screamed in defiance, and joy.

As the next wave pushed up into the gutter, it lifted me over the ledge again where I found a rock I could hold on to until the water had retreated, and I could come back to the real world. We were then free to walk away, pumped up with excitement and on a high. Sometimes, I felt anxious jumping into the incoming mass of water, but, as soon as I hit it, I had to concentrate as it carried me up and over the ledge. The timing, focus and skill needed to get both hands on the ledge left me no time for self-doubt, or fear.

When there was no surf, the rage hole provided the excitement that Greg and I, and our mates in the Lighthouse Road area, sought. We also engaged in a range of pranks that were sometimes very irresponsible and some illegal, with the police involved a couple of times but thankfully we were never charged. One of the more innocent activities we engaged in on long days when there was no surf, was the 'acid arse'. Our next door neighbour John had a dog called Peppy, that featured in this cruel punishment imposed on the younger boys in our group. With a strong northerly blowing, very little swell and nothing to do we were all looking for entertainment until someone said, "Been a while since we did an acid arse, boys." As possible victims, the younger boys became anxious and wary of any possible move to instigate this feared punishment. As the older boys exchanged subtle looks, the mood changed with all the younger boys mentally preparing to flee. At the call of "Honk!" from his older brother, Neil, he tried to escape but the boys beside him grabbed him and the others rushed to pin him down.

"No! No!" Honk screamed. "Let me go!" he pleaded as I backed Peppy toward him. "Not the acid arse!"

Sitting on Peppy, I supported my weight on my feet and made noises like a reversing truck as I backed him toward Honk. Holding Peppy's collar in my left hand, I used my right hand to lift his tail with his crusty anus hovering over Honk's face. Honk desperately threw his head from side to side until one of the boys held it still.

"Hurry up, Ric!" Neil shouted as I coaxed Peppy to sit until his anus touched Honk's horrified face.

"Acid arse!" I shouted as we sprinted away, pissing ourselves laughing with Peppy running beside us, barking excitedly and Honk rushing to wash his face under the nearest tap.

On the other side of us, the Walker family were heavily into horse racing and had a mare called Impedance who looked huge when being walked up to and back from her stable at the back of their property. They trained her on the beach and during the day kept her in a paddock about a kilometre away. The Walker boys talked me into having my first horse ride on Impedance in the paddock where she spent her days. When standing close to her and putting my hand on her, I realised how big she was and regretted agreeing to ride her. She was calm and had a pleasant smell as I tentatively stroked her, but I could sense her power.

"Go on, Ric, she'll be alright," Eric told me. "She'll just walk down nice and easy like she does every day. She's big but gentle. Don't worry about riding bareback. We'll give you a lift up."

I felt a long way up from the ground and, as I sat on her bareback with the reins in my hands, she felt warm against my legs and bum. I could feel each of her big breaths underneath me and did my best to look relaxed, but the Walker boys knew I was very anxious.

Impedance began walking like the Walker boys said she would but half-way down the small hill, she shifted up to a slow trot and headed for the barbed wire fence. Bouncing out of rhythm with her trot, I had no chance of slowing her down. Oh shit! I thought as we approached the fence where she propped and propelled me over it. Landing with a forward roll in the grass, I stood up with the Walker boys laughing, cheering, and clapping from a distance at the 'city boy' who had come to Byron Bay. I felt embarrassed, but glad that my first ride on a horse was over.

A couple of weeks after my ride on Impedance, I started school at Mullumbimby High School where I did not put much effort into my schoolwork but enjoyed playing rugby league for the school and strengthening my friendships with boys from the Bay. On Saturday nights I would walk into town to meet a few mates where we would watch fights in the top pub. Looking down from the footpath outside, we knew all the local boys in the pub and I had my heroes. Saturday night usually saw at least a couple of fights, fuelled by alcohol and anger with pushing and shoving, verbal abuse, and blood spilt. From a distance, it was entertaining but when the action was close, the brutality was confronting. During long spells of inaction at the top pub, some mates and I walked down Jonson Street and back looking for entertainment at the Great Northern Hotel (the middle pub). There were fights there as well that would spill out onto the footpath with the protagonists encouraged by a loud and drunken audience that followed them outside.

School was boring, but the train trips to and from school could be wild and entertaining. I even had a fist fight with a boy who lived near me on my first day of school, egged on by the students in the carriage. Neither one of us wanted to fight but we both gave in to the chants of the boys in the carriage to punch each other as the train rocked from side to side in a clumsy, ugly encounter that left me with sore spots on my head and face where he landed a couple of blows and sensitivity in my right fist where I had struck him in the head. It was a weird and even bizarre experience that felt wholly unnatural for me.

The students from Byron Bay travelled in the front carriages with the paying public behind us in the rear carriages. Sometimes, when the train stopped on the way home a few boys would quickly jump off to load large objects like pieces of metal and timber onto it. Later, when we crossed the Belongil Creek they threw them in the creek to splash water down the side of the train and into any open windows of paying passengers. I enjoyed watching this done and hooted with other boys when we thought we'd drenched a paying customer or two but was shocked when I found out what one of the Bay boys that I looked up to had done. Paul Haskew's father was so revered in the Byron Bay Surf Lifesaving club that he was referred to as Count Haskew, but his son Paul was a bit of a wild child. On the way to school, a local rebel, Paul Haskew dropped a turd into a paper cup and snuck down to one of the carriages for paying customers where he put it in a water cooler with a timber door. On a very hot summer day, and with the cooler not visible, it was not discovered until someone complained about the discoloured and awful tasting water. A few weeks later, Paul was expelled from school.

After being expelled, Haskew bought a blue Suzuki 200 Invader motorbike that he ripped around town on, and even ran into the school bus, leaving a long scratch down its lefthand side. Envious of Paul and dreaming of having my own motorbike, I spent my summer holidays that year working in Sydney to save up for one. My plan was to buy a Honda 175cc motor bike which would have been a sensible choice but when looking in a Brookvale bike shop, I saw an old Triumph 500. With lots of glistening chrome and its fuel tank painted metallic purple, I couldn't take my eyes off it and as soon as the salesman kick started it and revved it up inside the shop, I had to have it. My parents drove down to Sydney to help me buy a motorbike (advice and money) and my father told me not to buy the old Triumph because it was in poor condition and would cost me money, but I bought it. I rode my motorbike home to Byron Bay from Sydney with my parents following me in their car, and my father giving me a few breaks from the tiring vibration of the old bike. Back in Byron Bay, I had the biggest bike in town for a while and took many local girls for a spin on it. Feeling them pressed against me as I rode with my hair blowing in the wind and the roar of my bike in my ears was heaven for me.

Sometimes on a Friday night the local boys around my age who had motorbikes gathered for short, sharp drag races along Carlyle Street from Tennyson Street to Cowper Street. These occasional races were a real thrill for us and not just the racing with the danger of being caught by the police giving it an edge. Four to six bikes would usually be involved in one-on-one races that would be all over in about fifteen minutes. When it was my turn to race, I moved my bike into position, revving it up and totally focused on making the best start I could. Once my bike's muffler fell off and another time my headlight popped out when I missed a gear, but it was always fun and lots of thrills. The excitement was like what I felt at the rage hole but, this was a competition and I always wanted to win. We made a lot of noise racing up Carlyle Street in an otherwise very quiet town and it really must have annoyed the residents in that area. None of us fell off, and nobody was caught by the police, but they probably had a good idea who was involved.

What Do I Do Now?

Every summer powerful cyclones battered Byron Bay leaving marine debris, driftwood, and human rubbish on the beaches. When the cyclones had passed, Greg and I would run down to the beach to see what had been washed up, and one day we saw something big on Clarkes Beach.

"Wow!" Greg shouted. "Ric, what is that?"

"I don't know—let's have a look" I replied, and we sprinted toward it.

"It's the back of a surf boat!" he yelled as we approached it.

"Completely broken off," I said, putting my hand on it. I wondered where the rest of the boat was; maybe it was sunk? "But I reckon we can fix this," I added.

"Are you sure? It's really wrecked."

"We can put something across there and maybe row it backwards. We can do it for sure."

When John and another boy walking along the beach saw us, they jogged up to see what was going on. I told them we wanted to take it home and repair it.

"Really? How are you going to do that?" John said.

I explained my ideas with enough enthusiasm to convince them both. They then helped us drag and carry it home. Going up the steep sandy track was hard work, but we made it home to our backyard with what would become our summer project.

We had the stern of the boat with the timber fittings for two rowlocks, but the big challenge was how to repair and seal where it had broken off from the rest of the boat. With the stern narrow and tapered from where it had broken off, we cut a sheet of plywood to shape and evened up where the boat had split in two. The main problem for us was how to attach the plywood to create a new stern that would be waterproof. The plan was to make the original stern (back) the bow (front) and row it backwards.

We gouged bitumen softened by the heat of the summer sun

from the road to fill all the gaps and make our boat as waterproof as possible. It was a tedious task. Nobody really wanted to do the hard work like collecting bitumen so it could be forced it into gaps that would let water in.

I asked Greg, "Why don't you collect the tar, bring it quickly to me, and then I'll seal the gaps straight away?"

"That's not fair," he replied. "I'm not gunna do all the hard work out on the hot road while you just stay here."

"Well, it's supposed to be a bit of a team effort, isn't it?"

"No, you just want me to do a job you don't want to do."

We finally launched the boat in one of the large lagoons that formed on Clarke's Beach, but it was too high in the water and rolled over when we tried to get in. John fetched bags from his house that we filled with sand to put in the boat so that it sat lower in the water and one of Greg's mates, Mark, had a couple of oars in his garage that we used. After a successful test run in the lagoon, we tried it in the ocean on a very quiet day, and, one-by-one, we ironed out all the bugs and plugged the leaks which allowed us to use the boat over the remainder of that summer. When there was no surf, we would row out into the bay to snorkel on one of the nearest reefs.

I also used the boat to get to know a girl called Rhonda. A couple of times at school I had tried to catch her eye. The first two times she immediately looked down, but the third time she gave me a beautiful smile that lit up my day. She was not as outgoing or confident as the other girls I knew, but I was attracted to her quietness, and a sense of sadness she seemed to carry with her.

From time to time, I'd exchange a few words with her at the school canteen but not much more: "Hi, Rhonda."

"Hi, Ric, how are you?"

"Good, thanks."

I wanted to get to know her but had no idea how to do it. Rumour also had it that she lost her virginity to her next-door neighbour who was several years older than we were. He was also a bit of a rough character, and I didn't want to do anything to make him angry at me. But once the boat was finished and safe to use, I told her about it.

"Wow!" she said. "You guys are pretty clever. Where is it?"

"It's at our place, and we just usually row it in the lagoon at Clarkes. Would you like to have a go in it?"

"Yeah, I'd love to try it out. But only in the lagoon."

I was beside myself with excitement that day when I saw her walking along the beach toward me in her bikini as I was checking the boat for leaks.

"What do you think?" I said as she examined it.

"Looks good, but how do I get in?"

I pulled the boat closer to the sand so she could climb in, but she began to slip. I caught her arm, felt her soft, smooth skin, and didn't want to let go. Finally in the boat, she was wet with droplets of water glistening on her legs. I used an oar to push the boat off the sand, returned it to the rowlock and began to row. After a couple of strokes, I looked up to see her sitting there in front of me, like a goddess.

"Lucky we're only in the shallows with no chance of hitting an iceberg," I joked.

She laughed and said, "You're funny, Ric. What did you do on the weekends before you started on this boat?"

"Just surfing and sometimes going to the rage hole when there was a northerly."

I could feel my attraction to her growing and hoped that this would be the start of something with her, but I saw very little of her after she left school.

I played spin the bottle a couple of times when living on the Northern Beaches, but it all accelerated for me after we arrived in the Bay. My first experience of passionate kissing was in the hessian seats at the Brunswick picture theatre where reputations were made based on who had the longest, most passionate looking kisses. It was an intensely sensuous experience for me that made it difficult to sleep that night, as I lay in bed reliving the sensations of my encounters on the hessian seats. The feel of a girl's soft, moist lips against mine, her excitement, her scent, and the feel of her body against mine was mind blowing. If kissing could be so amazing how good must it be to have sex? I often thought.

My early interaction with girls included the conservative 'school social' at Mullumbimby High School. A band would play, with the boys sitting on one side of the hall and girls on the other. I really liked girls and was reasonably popular with them, but walking across an empty room to ask for a dance took a lot of courage. I'd try to look relaxed and confident but felt every eye in the room on me. I was only rejected once, but walking back was a crushing experience.I kept my head up, looked straight ahead, and tried to make a joke of it when I returned to the boys' side of the room. It was much more fun at the back of the bus on the way home to the Bay where the boys and girls partnered up for fumbling and clumsy sexual experiences on the way back to the Bay.

Mick Wills was a good-looking guy who was a charmer with the girls and my best mate during my early years at Mullumbimby high School. Within the first week of school, he introduced me to a couple of pretty girls and soon after school began, he pulled me aside at the canteen: "See that girl in the last line, with the long brown hair?"

"Yeah, I can see her."

"Do you fancy her at all?"

"She's pretty nice. Why?"

"She wants to fuck you."

"What?

"You heard what I said. Are you up for it?"

Filled with excitement and anxiety, I tried my best to look cool and avoid making it obvious that I had never done it. Mick told me Mary was experienced, which made me both excited and anxious about making some sort of mistake the first time I did it. Mick made the arrangements for me to meet Mary in Byron Bay one night, and I could think of little else all week.

After meeting awkwardly near the Council Chambers I suggested to Mary that we could do it inside the nearby fire station that I knew would not be locked. Excited, nervous, and clumsy, I lay down a piece of clothing that I found hanging up inside the fire station. She removed her delicate panties, lay on her back, and opened her legs. Overpowered by sexual desire, I began to panic as I fumbled in the dark with the condom. I ran outside where I sat on the curb under a streetlight to roll it on. I then quickly returned to where Mary was waiting. It was all soon over, and she stood up to adjust her clothing as though nothing had happened. I felt awkward yet satisfied at the same time, as we walked outside and said good night.

After my experience with Mary, I could not stop thinking about sex, and it started to compete with surfing for my attention. With most of my friends sexually active, we'd sometimes meet in someone's house when their parents were not there to pair up in a vacant bedroom, and, in my last year at school, I had my first sexual experience with an older woman.

Through my father's surfing connections, we hosted high profile surfer, Keith Paull, who won the 1968 national championships. I was so proud to be clambering over the slippery rocks behind him and was hoping someone I knew was watching.

Later, he took me to a party about two hundred metres up Lighthouse Road from our house. I was seventeen and the others at the party were all adults in their early to late twenties. I felt self-conscious walking in with everyone drinking, loud music and conversations.

Keith introduced me to a few people and then disappeared, leaving me to converse as best I could. When someone offered me whisky, I wanted to show I could handle it so I gulped it down. It burned my mouth and throat, and soon I felt my head spinning so much I had to sit down. I slumped back into an armchair and closed my eyes. An hour or more later, with the house empty and quiet, the woman who hosted the party woke me up with her hand on my shoulder. Blonde and confident, she had breasts that I had struggled not to look at all night before I passed out.

"I think you'd better have a shower before you go home to look presentable, if you know what I mean," she told me.

"You mean here?" I asked.

"Yes, you can't go home like that. Follow me, and I'll show you where the shower is. Come on."

We walked down the hall and turned into the bathroom. I was unsure how to respond until she turned the shower on, and gestured for me to get in.

I hesitated for a few seconds until she said, "You don't want to get your clothes wet, do you?"

After an awkward pause I stripped and got into the hot shower with my back to her and adjusted the temperature of the water hitting my face and chest. I expected her to close the shower door behind me and leave, but after about a minute I felt her behind me. I was suddenly a mess of emotions. Feeling her breasts against my back and her arms around me, I was aroused, intimidated and confused all at once. Having sex with her standing up was so surreal, and with the lingering effects of the whisky I had drunk, I thought

I might have been dreaming.

After we had dried ourselves and put our clothes back on, she wanted me to stay, but I knew I had to go home. I avoided my mother when I arrived, and the next day when she asked me what the party had been like, I didn't tell her what had happened.

When the party host called me at home a few nights later and asked me to come up while her partner was away because she was lonely, I told her I couldn't.

My mother had been listening and asked, "Who was that girl, Ric? She sounds very keen on you."

"Oh, just someone from school."

"What does she want?"

"She wants to meet up, but I told her I have to do my homework."

I later found out that my Mum knew her well, and that they regularly went to the beach together to sunbake.

That same year, a woman in her mid-twenties picked me up in the top pub.

"How old are you?" she asked while leaning on the bar and looking deep into my eyes, which I found a little intimidating.

"Eighteen," I said, when I was seventeen.

"That's too bad. I thought you were older."

"I'm old enough," I replied after sipping my beer, with as much macho confidence as I could muster.

We had sex in her Mini Minor, and over the next few weeks she picked me up once a week for sex in her car, but she suddenly disappeared.

Once I turned 17, I began sneaking into the top pub to experience what I had been watching from outside for three years. I looked young for my age, so I had to be careful and avoided staying too long. But about six months after turning 17, I found myself at a table of people I didn't know, sipping on a schooner of beer and listening to the band. Suddenly, I was floored by a king hit to the side of my head. I lay stunned on the concrete floor and not sure about what had just happened. The punch had been delivered by Steve, from Mullumbimby who had been a motorbike friend of mine until we had a falling out, he and some of his sidekicks sometimes tried to bully me. The guy sitting next to me took offence at the king hit and ripped into Steve. A brawl exploded above me.

Tables and chairs crashed around me, glasses smashed, and beer dripped off the tables above me as I crawled out to escape with the bouncers rushing to the melee.

Not long after the king hit, I came across a pamphlet on karate. It had a couple of self-defence moves and instructions on how to toughen my knuckles for devastating punches. For a couple of weeks, I practised the self-defence moves against an imaginary attacker and pounded a wooden box filled with sand that I later replaced with fine gravel. The room Greg and I shared was part of an extension at the back of the house and, when punching the box of sand, I could hear my father's footsteps as he approached so quickly hid the sand box in my cupboard and rushed to my desk with homework on it and look as studious as I could.

Over the latter half of the Sixties, surfing was at the centre of my life, I became obsessed with sex, but I enjoyed the thrills of roof rocking. Saturday night, after hanging around in town and watching fights we had two options for going home. The fastest route was along the beach and up the sandy track to home. The option of walking up Carlyle Street to the top shop and turning left down Massinger Street to Lighthouse Road took longer but offered opportunities for rocking roofs, and we didn't rock just any roof.

We rocked the roofs of houses occupied by people who we felt deserved it, like the owner of a successful electrical business in town (he was unfairly rich) and the old man next to Haskew's house because he was cranky and unpleasant. Then there was the family who lived on a hill near the town reservoir. We sometimes saw the mother in town wearing what looked like a black geisha wig and when her son found a load of pink undercoat paint at the dump, they painted the entire house pink. This made it an irresistible target.

After deciding to rock the pink house one Saturday night, Neil, Barry, and I talked tactics as we walked up Massinger Street. Not a word was spoken as we searched for rocks of the appropriate size and shape under a clear night sky and a big moon. I would hold each rock in my hand with a bit of movement up and down to assess its weight and how right it felt. Once we'd set ourselves up with a small pile of rocks each and adjusted our throwing stances, we were ready to go. I caught the eye of the other two boys and we launched our assault on the pink house before bolting off into the night as the rocks rattled down the roof behind us. My heart pumped as we sprinted away from the house. When a single gunshot echoed in the night, we hit top speed until we felt far enough away from the house to stop.

"Holly shit—they shot at us!" Neil gasped. "Is everyone OK?"

"What the hell do they think they are doing? We should go to the police and dob in the mad bastards." Barry replied.

"You're going to tell the cops we rocked their roof?" I responded as I caught my breath. "I don't think so. That's got to be the end of rocking that bloody house."

We were never caught rocking roofs until a few school mates, and I rocked the roof of my science teacher in Year 12. Chemical Ken was an unpopular science teacher I disliked very much, and he disliked me just as much. After he had been particularly unfair to me, a group of the Year 12 boys agreed to give him a massive stoning on the coming Friday night with seven to eight boys 'definitely' committing to turn up, and a couple of maybes.

I was first to arrive at the meeting point on the peak of the hill above Ken's house. After 10 minutes, two more boys turned up but, after another 20 minutes had passed, it looked like no one else would join us. It was a risky idea to stone the science teacher's roof and we had lost the safety in numbers we expected to have but, I was keen to go ahead anyway. Ken lived in an 'A frame' house on the side of a hill, and we were standing above it. One of the boys was ambivalent but the other seemed happy to go ahead with the rocking. Looking down on Ken's roof glowing in the moonlight, it seemed to beckon to us.

"That roof's asking to be rocked, and he deserves it, doesn't he?" I said.

"Okay, let's do it," one kid said with the other nodding in agreement.

I stood in a side-on throwing stance with a rock in my hand and others on the ground at my feet as I adjusted my stance. I took a deep breath and at the nod of my head, the three of us began hurling rock after rock at Ken's roof. The sound of waves of rocks hitting the steep roof and rattling down it shattered the silence of the night excited us as we worked ourselves into a rocking frenzy. Just as we finished our barrage Ken ran outside to confront us: "What the hell are you doing? I am going to call the police!"

"Fuck you, Ken!" I shouted at him before throwing a couple more rocks in defiance and disappearing into the darkness. He had no chance of catching us, but he didn't need to. Knowing full well who had attacked his house, he contacted the principal, and we were expelled on Monday. Later, when I had calmed down, I realised how immature and reckless I had been.

My father was furious. "What is wrong with you, Ric? How stupid can you be? Of course, he knew who it was."

"Sorry, I wasn't thinking very well."

"The worst thing for me is that I can't stand the bastard, but now, I have to apologise to him for what *you* did. I have to kiss his bloody arse because you were so bloody stupid!"

"Sorry."

"You'll pay for this, Ric."

After some investigation, my father found out that Ken had a history of similar problems at previous schools and took his case to the principal. A few days later, we were reinstated, but I had to sell my surfboard to pay my share of the costs involved in replacing the damaged roof. It was very awkward in Ken's chemistry classes for the rest of the year, and that was my last rocking.

Later that year, with my results from the 1969 HSC (High School Certificate) being very poor, I had few options for further education but had convinced myself that it didn't matter. Deep down, I was disappointed with how poorly I had done but did not want to face it, and the fact that I hadn't put any effort in. Back in primary school at Avalon, the principal had called my parents in to point out that I had a high IQ but was doing poorly. For my last year at primary school, he put me in class taught by a male teacher who was also coach of the school rugby league team, the mighty Sparrows. I loved playing in the Sparrows over a very successful season and my grades picked up. When I went to Pittwater High School, I was placed in high level classes but with no one watching over me, dropped to the bottom level classes in most subjects. The same thing happened when we moved to Byron Bay, and I enrolled in Mullumbimby High School.

There were few possibilities for any post-secondary studies for me, and I just wanted to escape to a life of fun and freedom. With school finished and nothing in front of me I was lost for what to do next until some mates I kept in touch with from the northern beaches in Sydney turned up at our home in two panel vans. They had also finished school that year and were doing a surfing safari up to Byron Bay via Crescent Head and Angourie, as a well-established surfers' journey. I decided to follow them back to Sydney.

With my family gathered in the front yard to say goodbye, I was torn between staying in my warm home and moving to Sydney to enjoy an adventurous life. By this time, Greg and I were calling our father by his first name of Bill and, using both Betty and Mum for our mother. Bill had forgiven me for being such a loser in my last year at school, making so little effort and getting into trouble so much. I think he was confident, or at least hopeful, that I would eventually realise my academic potential and find some direction. Mum's last, long hug was full of love and stayed with me for the first hour on my bike. As I rode, I was anxious about what I was leaving behind but over the next half an hour, on I felt increasingly excited about what was in front of me. Vibrating badly, my bike was a disaster waiting to happen and blew up halfway through the trip. My mates and I had to squeeze it into the back of a panel van for the rest of the journey, and that is how I made my start to my post school life in Sydney.

Living with friends in a house at North Curl Curl, I had six menial jobs that ranged from working in a small pie heater factory at Brookvale to swinging a mattock and shovelling for Warringah Shire Council. Paying my share of the rent and food, the cost of going out on the weekend and paying for my bike to be repaired left me with nothing at the end of the week, but I was very happy when it was finished. I was mobile and my friend from primary school at Avalon, Neil (Ned), had a motor bike as well. Cruising around Manly Vale on a Friday night we saw two attractive girls sitting at a bus stop. I pulled up a little further up the road and spoke to Neil when he stopped.

"They're hot, Ned. Let's go back and offer them a ride home."

"Are you sure, mate?" he asked. "I'm pretty sure they'll knock us back."

"Come on, Ned. It's worth a try."

"Okay, if you're keen."

After a quick U-turn we pulled over on the left-hand side of the road to make another U-turn. With Ned in front of me I was looking back for a break in the traffic and, when I saw one, I accelerated quickly, to smash into the back of his bike. After disentangling our bikes, I planted my side stand on the grass and it sunk into the soft ground to send my bike and me down the grass incline. Ned helped me get my bike back up on the road. We'd forgotten about the girls as we struggled to get my bike up the embankment but looked up to see them looking down at us and smiling as they departed on the bus.

I opened the letter from the NSW Department of Education with some anticipation and was elated to see an offer for a place in the teachers' college at Lismore that I had applied for. It was 45 mins from Byron Bay, so I immediately rang my parents to tell them that I was coming home, and was going to be a teacher.

Finding Meaning and Direction

College offered an escape from the harsh reality of working to survive and I loved it. Hundreds of young people like me released from the control of their parents with the number of first year pregnancies the biggest concern for the college. My time was devoted to endless social events, mixing with lively, happy girls, drinking and smoking weed. Some classes put me to sleep, but I enjoyed those that encouraged creativity and provided opportunity for expression. This included pottery, poetry, creative writing and drama where a small group of us would get stoned before classes and entertain the lecturer. I re-joined the Byron Bay rugby (union) club and was later selected in the Far North Coast representative team to compete in the NSW Country Championships. Travelling to Sydney to compete at that level was exciting, and in one game I marked the Wallabies' scrum half at the time and played well.

I failed so many courses in my first semester that I was told to come back the next year to retake them. Not again, I thought, when I read my results. Personal disappointment and dread of how disappointed my father would feel swept over me but there was nothing I could do. Even if he could be understanding or forgiving, I had screwed up again and did not seem to be learning anything.

Over what was semester two for my friends at college, I worked as a deckhand on a trawler moored in Brunswick Heads, under the command of 'Captain Bligh'. He would pick me up at around 4.30 pm and dropped me back home at about 7.30 am the next day.

Chugging out over the bar at the mouth of the Brunswick River for the first time, I looked forward to the adventure that awaited me. It was a real buzz for me and a touch of adventure for the first week, but as it became routine, I grew tired of it. I also reflected a little on what a loser I could become if I could not learn to get the job done, whatever it was. I did not seem to be able to apply myself to anything that looked like work. Working all night, the smell of prawns, diesel, and other sea life we killed, with only short bouts of sleep, made being a deck hand hard work. One of us would steer the boat while the other slept for thirty to forty minutes. When it was time, we would pull the nets up, dump the load of sea life we had ripped up from the floor of the ocean and 'sort' it. I had to put the prawns down one chute, and the rest out another chute, directly back into the ocean. God help me if I sent one prawn down the wrong chute.

Sharks feeding on scraps followed the boat all night and I could see flashes of them under the light hanging from the mast. With the boat rolling in the black sea, the low gunnels were all there was keeping me dry and safe. The captain opened the net to release things that sting, bite, and even give electric shocks into a seething mass of panicking sea life on the sorting tray. A small shark about a metre long dropped out of the net and thrashed violently on the tray. I had seen the captain throw similar sized sharks back in the ocean but froze until he screamed at me.

"Toss that fuckin' thing back it the water! Grab it by its fuckin tail! Go on!"

I watched the shark hit the water and indulged in a few seconds of satisfaction, until he yelled at me again:

"Do you think he's gunna jump back in the fuckin' boat? Get your arse over here. We've got work to do."

Sometimes we were at sea for two to three nights and would moor up in Queensland at places like Amity Point on North Stradbroke Island. I couldn't get my hair clean washing in saltwater with dish washing liquid and was always worried about sharks. The prawns were cooked on board, but we never ever ate one. Never. I tried to grab 40 minutes sleep with the boat rocking from side to side, the drone of the engine, the stench of prawns, other sea life, and diesel. Just as I seemed to fall asleep, Captain Bligh would wake me up by turning on the light and yell, "wakey, wakey, hand off snaky!"

In my second attempt at college, my English lecturer, Maurie Ryan, was also coach of the college first XV rugby team and a long-time stalwart of College Rugby. In my first class with him, he recognised my name while checking the roll.

"Ric Light?"

"Yes."

"Used to play rugby for Byron Bay."

"I still do."

"Not if you want to pass this subject."

Playing rugby for College pitted me against my brother when we played Byron Bay, because, at sixteen, he had joined the Byron Bay rugby club. He played rugby league at school with boys his own age but was prepared to step up on Saturdays to play rugby against men twice his age and older. Determined to succeed, he asked Bill to teach him how to tackle. Bill was more than happy to work with Greg and spent many hours in our backyard tackling him and having Greg tackle him. He asked me if I would like to join them when I was home, but I was not interested.

From the first game of the rugby season, Greg's determined defence earned him respect on the Byron Bay team. He had become a punishing defender who enjoyed cutting ball carriers in half. Starting on the wing early in his first season, he later moved into the centres as he adapted to the game and playing with men. I usually played scrumhalf, but the first time Byron Bay played College that season we both played inside centre. This offered Greg a golden opportunity to demonstrate his tackling prowess on me, and he was primed for the encounter. He was looking forward to showing Bill how much he had learned and scoring a few points in our brotherly rivalry.

Early in the game, Greg didn't have many opportunities, but I was aware of him coming at me every time. He'd come up a little too quickly and a touch too wide, which allowed me to step inside him and make a break.

Later, he evened the score when he hit me hard in the ribs and we both went to ground. I said nothing, and I didn't look him in the eye as he already knew he'd got the better of me.

"Nice tackle, Greg," one of the Byron Bay players called out with a look in my direction.

In the second half, Greg moved inside to tackle our number 10 but not before he'd passed the ball to me. This created a gap that I ran through, drew the fullback, and then passed to a support player who scored. I made sure I caught Greg's eye after that little victory and smiled, but I knew he would be desperate for revenge. Toward the end of the game, he hammered me so hard that I dropped the ball and stayed on the ground for a short time to recover.

My old Byron Bay teammates were very vocal with their congratulations for Greg's big hit. "Good one, Lighty," "You smashed him, Greg," "Go the Bay!"

I finally stood up, looked Greg in the eye and said, "Nice one, Chidley" (a nick name of his), with a nod that he'd won that encounter.

"I just don't like seeing you two boys hurting each other," Betty told us after the game "I worry about you getting hurt."

But Bill was excited. He congratulated both of us on playing well and had a dig at me by saying, "Great tackle on your brother, Greg."

"Yeah, well done, Chidley," I replied but with far less enthusiasm than Bill.

I didn't admit it to Greg, but I was impressed with his tackling. I also had thoughts about him having more long-term commitment and determination to achieve goals he set for himself than I did.

"Ric... maybe you'd be interested in a couple of sessions in the backyard to improve your tackling?" said Bill.

Greg laughed, and I managed a smile. So did Betty, but in a demure way with a gentle nod that only she could do.

At college, I shared a house where my flatmates and I smoked quite a bit of dope and regularly played guitar and sang together. I also thoroughly enjoyed working as a co-editor for the college newspaper with my friend Kev who played rugby for the college firsts rugby team. I enjoyed the opportunity for creativity it offered and for sharing ideas with someone I clicked with. We would get stoned and piss ourselves laughing as we compiled what we thought were hilarious criticisms of the college leadership. Kev's drawings were superb and made us laugh even more. The last edition we created was seen to be so offensive by the Dean of Men and the Principal that all copies were confiscated and placed in the dean's office. Kev and I were able to get into his office when the Dean was out and recover them for distribution, but that was the end of us editing the college newspaper.

I received my notice of appointment to a school in the mail and was pleased that I had finally going to be teacher and had been appointed to a school. I would be Teacher-in-Charge at Colo Heights Public School but was unsure how to react because I didn't know where it was.

"Here it is!" Bill announced, finding it on a map of NSW.

"In the middle of nowhere, Ric! Greg called out after rushing to see where it was on the map. "Hillbilly country!"

It was a one teacher school northwest of Sydney, 56 kilometres up the Putty Road from Windsor and 93 kilometres by road from the Sydney, CBD.

Two petrol stations formed the social and financial centre of the community. At the one where I checked in, the owner gave me the keys to the school and told me where it was. He also told me that I would drive the school bus to pick up all the children before school and drop them off after school.

"You'll be staying with Muriel Ward," he told me.

"Do I have a choice?"

"No, not really," he said with a big smile.

"Are there any flats or houses I could rent?"

He and the young man working in the shop with him looked at each other and laughed politely with the owner shaking his head and saying, "No, sorry, that's it. That's where the teacher always stays."

Muriel was a direct descendent of the infamous bushranger, Thunderbolt Ward, who operated on the New England tablelands and there were no options for accommodation. It seemed the teacher always stayed with Muriel.

I drove down a kilometre or so from the service station to see where I would start my career as a teacher. I felt each of the six solid timber steps under my feet, opened the door and walked into the empty, dusty room. Standing in the middle of the classroom, I paused to soak it all in and thought, this is where I am going to teach tomorrow. From facing the blackboard, I turned toward the desks and chairs where I imagined a room full of children. It was the first time I had fully felt the weight of responsibility as the only teacher in the school.

The next day, I drove over rough dirt roads surrounded by bush to pick up most of the 33 children on the regular school bus run and pulled up in front of the classroom. They poured out onto the school ground, and straight into what must have been their usual morning activities.

After walking into the classroom to set up what I thought I needed for my first class, I stopped and looked around the room. Suddenly, I realised how unprepared I was and how my plan to play it as it comes was probably not going to work. At nine o'clock, I called out to the students to line up in front of the small deck that I stood on for the first assembly and to formally introduce myself.

"Good morning, everyone. My name is Mr Light, and I am your new teacher. You don't know me, and I don't know you, but I will get to know you as soon as I can. We are all going to have a great year and I am looking forward to teaching you."

Every day, I devoted time to singing, games and gardening because they were easier to teach to a big group with such a wide range of ages. I also believed in the importance of happiness in the classroom. My guitar was central to my teaching, and I reached for it when the flow of the day was interrupted, or when things looked like falling apart. It saved me so many times and every morning we made a positive start to the day by singing a few songs that the students chose from our growing repertoire.

Greg came down to visit me in my first year, spent every day at my school and loved it. He played guitar, sang with the children, and had them make cardboard guitars that they pretended to strum as he played, and they all sang. He played sport with them, watched all my teaching, and taught a few small groups for me. His experience at my school confirmed his desire to be a teacher, so he applied for entry into a Bachelor of Teaching at the University of New England. That was the university Greg wanted to attend but he was a little short of the required UAI (University Admission Index) score so repeated year 12. It was embarrassing for him, but he swallowed his pride and went back to school when his mates were off to university. The next year, he was admitted into the teacher education program he wanted to be in.

At Colo Heights, my class and I sang in the morning after recess, after lunchtime and any other time we needed a song as well as playing a lot of games. Teaching was very challenging for the first few weeks, but I gradually adapted and profited from some telephone conversations with my father. Despite being a little lost teaching students from ages five to fourteen in the one room, I enjoyed every day. After the students sang each morning, it was time for 'show and tell' which was always entertaining but sometimes provided insights into family lives that I was not ready for. My response varied from having to cut short the story being told because it was inappropriate to finding it very funny. From an "Okay, thank you, Jimmy. Thanks for that and you can sit down now," to most of the class and me breaking into uncontrollable laughter and me saying "Very funny, Maria. I think everybody enjoyed that very much."

At the beginning of the year, one of the older boys stood up for show and tell holding a small snake that he said he had captured in the bush over the barbed wire fence. He held the squirming snake below its head while he explained to the class how he caught it and that it was not venomous.

"Put that outside now, Bradley," I told him.

"Yes, Mr Light," he said and headed toward the door but as he began to open it, he dropped the snake. It took off out the door with the younger children screaming over the clatter of their tables and chairs, and the older ones laughing.

After a few conversations with Bill over the phone about the many challenges I faced, I started to settle in and adjust to the responsibilities and opportunities of teaching in such an unexpected environment. I came to really enjoy helping my students learn while having fun with them and providing opportunities for creativity.

After two weeks of heavy rain abated, I decided to drive the school bus I kept at home to a pub in Richmond, which was 40 kilometres away. I took the back road route home and as I drove toward the Colo River, turned left, and headed down to cross the bridge. Just as my headlights picked up the bridge the bus suddenly sunk into the deep silt and mud left behind by the flood. The rear wheels spun but it didn't not move. What an idiot! In the middle of the night, and in the depths of the dark, desolate valley, I was bogged in the school bus. It took me a few minutes to think about what I could do and realised that I would have to call the owner of the bus and tell him what a dick head I'd been. But first I had to find a phone.

With no streetlights, I walked for about ten minutes before I saw a house, but its lights were off. I approached it anyway and as I neared the door; I thought back to a similar experience earlier that year when I ran out of petrol on the Putty Road one night. The car spluttered and the engine stopped, so I put the car into neutral and coasted to a safe part of the road where I pulled over. I had passed a house earlier so walked back to it to ask for enough petrol to get me to the next petrol station. After knocking on the door, I stood and waited on the porch. I heard someone walk toward me and stop at the door, but no lights came on, so I began to feel uneasy. I heard the doorknob turn and the squeak of the door slowly opening. My feeling that something was wrong gave way to raw fear as the twin barrels of a shot gun pointed at my chest slowly emerged from the darkness. Time stopped for a moment, until a deep, threatening voice said: "Fuck off."

"Okay, no problem," I replied as I slowly backed away and the door closed.

I knocked on the door of the house in Colo Valley with no lights on a few times and waited in the darkness, but nobody answered, so I walked for fifteen minutes to the next house. Apologising profusely, I told them I was the local teacher and explained my situation. They opened the door and let me in to call the owner of the bus who owned one of the service stations on Colo Heights. I walked back to the bogged bus and only had to wait ten minutes for the tow truck to arrive. The owner did not have much to say as I sat in silence beside him and from then on, I had to leave the school bus at his service station when I had finished my school run.

Re-establishing my social networks around the northern beaches of Sydney over weekends allowed me to add some spice to the annual school social event that the teacher always organised. Every year, the school community organised a small band of locals to play politely in the hall, but I wanted to do something different.

I convinced friends of mine who had a rock band, to travel from the northern beaches to play in the local hall for free. There was a lot of interest from the children and their parents who had gathered to see the band arrive and set up. The microphones, the drum kit and the big speakers looked out of place in the old hall. It all looked very loud, and it was. The students loved it, but the older people didn't. Initially, they sat inside the hall as they had done each year before to my arrival but did not stay long. I could see a few heads shaking in disapproval as they left the hall and walked away.

With some financial help from my parents, I put down a deposit on a new Ducati 750cc motorbike. I was besotted with it and polished it every night in Muriel's garage for the first month or two. Every weekend, I rode my bike to Newport on the northern beaches to stay with a friend. Chris lived with his partner Robyn and was also into bikes. From Newport, we would take a ride on Saturday or Sunday to places like Gosford or down to Wollongong, and I would get back to Colo Heights late Sunday night, or early Monday morning.

Intoxicated by the power in my right hand and the deep growl of my big V-twin Ducati, I carved smooth lines through every corner at Bayview with the water glistening under the bright sun to my right. I felt on top of the world and, with Chris in front of me, decided to show off by going inside him as we approached the next corner. Laying my Ducati over, I passed Chris and began to accelerate through the corner until the road suddenly disappeared as the corner turned back inside itself. My bike ground into the asphalt and the rear tyre lost its grip. I slid across onto the other side of the road and smashed into a guidepost. In an instant, I went from pleasure to agony as my left knee exploded and my bike hit the mangroves.

I tried to stand up but collapsed in excruciating pain and fell into a foetal position. Curled on the side of the road, I could see my broken patella jutting out through my torn and blood-soaked jeans. People crowded around me trying to help and asking if I was okay, but I couldn't answer as I struggled with the pain until I recognised Chris's voice. He sounded like he had everything under control.

"You'll be okay, Ric. Can you hear me?"

When I nodded, he added, "Good. We'll get you in a car and on your way to Mona Vale hospital. I'll look after your bike."

In too much pain and shock to talk, I just nodded again.

He had someone help him put me in the back of a car and drive me to the hospital with him arriving soon after. Waiting at the hospital for pain killing drugs was the most painful experience of my life as I begged for an injection. The high that followed made me feel good enough to laugh and make jokes with my friends, but the pain gradually returned.

My recovery after the bike accident took longer than it should have because my patella broke again one day when I kicked a rugby ball at school.

"You've torn it asunder," the orthopaedic surgeon in Dee Why told me on what was supposed to be my last appointment.

With my leg in a cast for such a long time, the muscles in my left leg wasted. I had moved out of Muriel's house into a small tin shed built on a concrete slab, dug into the side of a steep hill, and overlooking a valley with a narrow, dirt road leading down to it. When I met the guy living on the other side of the hill, with his girlfriend and German Shepherd, he told me about a karate club in the Windsor boat shed that he had recently joined. I went to check it out and liked it so much that I decided to sign up.

When I started karate at the Windsor Boat Shed, I found it challenging due to my weak left leg and inflexibility. I couldn't kick above knee height but enjoyed it and stuck with it. I had never applied myself to anything like this before and was encouraged by getting results. Month by month, my leg became stronger, I became more flexible, and karate became the focus of my life. I started by going to one class a week but by my second year was training four nights a week and on Saturdays and karate gave my life more meaning than I had experienced before. My motivation came from being able to set and achieve the short-term goals of gaining the next coloured belt on the way toward black belt and by the feeling of internal positive satisfaction and physical change. The very clear, strong values of karate also appealed to me as I started reading about Karate, other martial arts and the samurai. I felt like I was beginning to enter a different world.

Even though contact was limited in karate classes, sparring was initially unnerving for me as I faced people that I didn't know and had to face my fears but week by week I developed confidence and skill. When I first began sparring all I could see was a blur of fists and feet coming at me but gradually made sense of it and saw the gaps I could attack. I soon came to enjoy sparring the most and would sometimes get a little too aggressive as I began to feel released from the restriction of fear and self-doubt. One night when I was too aggressive in sparring at the Windsor club, the head of the organisation grabbed me by the top of my *gi* (karate uniform) behind my neck and slung me into a stack of chairs.

"Wind down!" he yelled at me.

A few months after I had started training and had a grading, my neighbour with the German Shepard suggested we do some sparring down in the valley that my shed overlooked.

"What about us doing a bit of sparring or something out here somewhere, Ric?"

"What, outside? Not in class?"

"Yeah, a bit of extra training. The more we spar, the better we'll get."

"Where would we do it?"

"I reckon down there in the valley. There's lot of flat space near the creek."

Step by step, the gravel crunched under my shoes as we walked down the narrow, dusty road without a word exchanged. At the bottom of the valley and not another person in sight I wondered if this was really happening. Stretching in the silence and thick heat, I thought about how the encounter might develop. Would it be friendly, controlled, and respectful sparring or develop into a fight that did not finish until one of us was knocked out? Or even dead?

There was no turning back now, so I decided to initiate the first move. "Let's make a start."

"Sure, let's do it," he replied, as he moved quickly and confidently into the space we had agreed to use.

After bowing to each other, we took our stances and stared into each other's eyes.

He quickly came toward me with an attack that I dodged as we repositioned ourselves. He threw a front kick that I blocked as I move backwards then tried to counter with a punch but did not find the target. From there on the intensity built with some hard body blows delivered on both sides. I took a strong front kick to my abdomen that I really felt but did not react to. This was not the controlled sparring I was used to in the *dojo*. It seemed to be developing into an aggressive, and possibly brutal contest of will and strength with the sounds of our *kiai* resonating within the rocky valley with each encounter.

No matter how hard he came at me, I did not waver. I repelled his attack and looked for gaps in his defence as he came in at me or when regaining his mental and physical readiness. The increasingly strong blows I took to my body did not hurt or slow me down as I felt myself becoming more deeply immersed in the encounter. My initial fear and anxiety gave way to increasing confidence and tuning into the rhythm and flow of the sparring. I had butterflies in my stomach before we started but not now. I didn't feel angry or scared but instead, focused and in the moment.

Our sparring session seemed to last a long time, but it was probably no more than two to three minutes. I began with a mindset of surviving and defending but after several clashes, developed enough confidence to launch my own attacks.

I can do this, I thought, and from that point on began to get the upper hand.

After one further intense encounter, he turned his back on me and walked away. "That's enough, I'm done," he said, gesturing with his hand that it was over. I was relieved it had finished before it got ugly. It did a lot for my confidence because I thought he was a much stronger and more aggressive man than I was.

In conversation a month or so after our encounter, he told me how he had jumped bail on an armed robbery charge. "I'd rather die than go back inside," he told me.

That is why he took up karate. He, his girlfriend, and his German Shepherd disappeared not long after this conversation, and a little later I moved out of my corrugated iron shack on the side of the hill and into a farmhouse in the Colo Valley with two friends I had made through karate. Dave ran the farm and trained once or twice a week, and Dick was a mechanic who was more committed to karate and trained up to four times a week.

Learning to Commit and Take Risks

A high-profile martial artist from Hong Kong and son of a renowned kung fu grand master, Chan Cheuk Fai, inspired me the first time I saw him teaching and demonstrating technique. I had never seen anyone so skilful and was very nervous when I first sparred with him.

At this stage of my karate journey, I was getting good results in tournaments, but was not in the same world as Chan Cheuk Fai. I noticed him wearing only one sparring mitt for his lead hand as he shifted from the person who he had been sparring toward me. We bowed, and there he was in front of me. I did my best but using only one gloved hand, he just played with me. I did not come anywhere near landing a punch or kick on him but gave it my best. After our sparring, we bowed and before he moved on to the next person, he gave me a pat on the shoulder that meant a lot to me.

After his visit to the same *dojo* the next week and with the help of the boss of the karate school, I invited him to the farmhouse I shared with Dick and Dave for a few days. The old farmhouse in a desolate valley and beside the Colo River was a long way from Hong Kong and the inner city where Cheuk Fai was living. The three of us were in awe of him for the first couple of hours at the farm but his sense of humour helped all of us all relax, laugh, and enjoy his company. The mini karate tournaments we had in the living room with him as referee were hilarious and the highlight of his visit for me. His visit encouraged me to lighten up a bit with my attitude to karate and my need to stop being so hyper competitive. Being more relaxed also improved my sparring and hand speed.

After moving up a couple of grades, I was travelling to other *dojo* to train and improve in open karate tournaments with my most satisfying achievement being as a member of the team that competed in the NSW state team titles. The head of our karate system had picked his A team, and I was not in it, but, when I met the others in the B team, we clicked. All highly motivated with great camaraderie and wanting to show the boss he picked the wrong A-team we kept on winning until we found ourselves in the final. With five in each team and all having fought, it was a draw that would be decided by one extra bout. We had to choose one of us to decide fight on the deciding bout and I had won my bout but was anxious about letting the team down.

While I was trying to decide whether to put my hand up or not, one of my teammates stood up, to say "I'll do it." I was relieved, and he won the deciding bout to clinch the state title for the B team. We all celebrated, and I was on a high for a couple of days. I was later selected in an Australian team to fight against the Japanese national team in Sydney at Martin Place. I lost my bout but knew I had done the best I could. I wound down my need to win, did my best and refused to be intimidated which helped me get in touch with my inner self and learn a little.

Dick trained as much as I did and most nights of the week after training, we would sit around the kitchen table with Dave, talking about life, our dreams, and karate. During one of these discussions, I suggested we set a goal for ourselves.

"We are all brown belts, right? It won't be long before we can go for our black belt grading, and I've been thinking about something. Why don't we all get up to the last level before blackbelt, go to Hong Kong to get our blackbelts and then come back to open a *dojo* in Byron Bay?"

"Byron Bay?" Dick asked. "What are we going to do there, and how will we find the money to survive?"

"We set up a *dojo* and teach, say three nights a week, to bring in the money. There are no martial arts at all in Byron Bay and I reckon the locals would love it. We'll have packed classes every night."

"Well, I guess that's possible," was Dave's reply. "It's kind of a pretty good idea but I'm not sure how soon I can get a black belt."

Dick and Dave then looked at each other and nodded.

'Just imagine it, boys,' I went on. 'We would live the good life of surfing, meeting beautiful women during the day and teaching karate at night. Surfing, sex, and karate. We'll open a club in Byron Bay and could even start a club in another town and pull in more money. The nearest other karate club is an hour's drive away. What do you think?"

"Well, I can't surf, but it sounds good to me, Ric." said Dave.

"Yeah, why not?" Dick added with enthusiasm as he passed the joint to me. "I don't know much about Byron Bay, but why can't we do it? We could even set up a big tournament and clean up. I'm in!"

With the Colo Heights school student numbers growing enough to need an extra teacher, I contacted a college mate from Grafton and suggested he apply. From Grafton, Leon was living in Sydney but thinking about where he wanted his children to grow up. He applied and was appointed as my assistant teacher. The number of students continued to rise, and I was told that one of us had to move on so, I spoke to Leon at recess.

"Leon, I've been told that enrolments will keep increasing, so they have to appoint someone senior to run the school.

"Oh… so does that mean you have to leave?"

"No. Not necessarily. It can be either one of us. What would you do if you had the choice?"

"Ric, I've got a family, and we only just moved here so…. If I had a choice, I'd like to stay here but it's probably up to you as Teacher-in-Charge."

I felt for him and was hoping to get a school closer to Byron Bay so volunteered to move but was given a position in a primary school near the air force base in Richmond, 52 kilometres south of Colo Heights.

After the freedom of being in charge and the adventures I had at Colo Heights, the new school felt constraining. The conservative deputy principal had the room next to me and started every day with his class reciting maths tables. With very little interaction, his students all quietly did what they were told. He complained about my class singing, a group of children broadcasting selections of music at lunch time, and me taking them outside too much for physical education. This was something I had to adapt to but, on the other hand, teaching a class of children all the same age was much easier than teaching at Colo Heights. I soon clicked with my Year Five students who picked up on my enthusiasm and sense of humour. Every day, I enjoyed a few good laughs with them, but I never heard the deputy principal's class laugh. They seemed dull and compliant to me.

"You need to start each day by drilling the class with their tables to settle them down and get them ready for learning."

"I understand that, but I want my students to have fun and enjoy learning, and that's why I start with singing. I want to start each day in a positive way."

"You only have so many hours in a school day, Richard, so use every minute to teach them. They can run around, play, and sing outside at recess and lunchtime."

Once my students understood me, we had a ball, and I enjoyed every day but often had to defend my teaching and views on learning. The deputy principal didn't like my teaching approach, and I was not popular with the principal either.

I had a fascinating boy in my class I refer to as Liam, who insisted that he was from Mars. He could provide every detail of how he got to earth, how the earthlings who appeared to be his parents were just looking after him between his trips back to Mars. He was a very imaginative and creative boy with a good story and a cheeky smile.

When talking about Mars-related things at show and tell, Liam would sometimes speak in Martian language (that is what he said it was). The rest of the class were always keen to grill him with questions, but he always had solid answers that allowed him to sit down with his story intact. He was more of a nerd than a sporty type but enjoyed the daily PE classes, and I met his parents who were very nice people and had no problem with his Mars fixation.

Liam entered the annual school cross country and trained for it, but I thought he would be lucky to finish. On the day of the event, he turned up in a T-shirt he made to look like he was sponsored by Mars Bars. I had a giggle when I saw him and congratulated him on his sponsorship. Later, I congratulated him on finishing in the top three, which was an amazing result. He was not just another brick in the wall and had some sort of special energy. He was intelligent, positive, happy, creative, and refused to be ordinary.

One morning, the principal called me to his office before class to tell me that he had found Liam in his toilet. When asked to explain why he was there, Liam told the principal he had been to Mars but when beamed back to earth, had missed the target. Apparently, he kept a straight face when explaining why he was in the principal's toilet, but I am sure he couldn't have stopped at least, the hint of a cheeky smile on his face.

Later, I asked him, "What did you say to the principal when he asked you why you were in his toilet?"

"I said that there was a mistake when I was beamed back from Mars, and I missed the target."

"Did he believe you?"

"No. He said 'You can't be serious. I asked you, what were you were doing in my toilet?'"

"OK, thanks, Liam, and don't let that happen again."

"Yes, Mr Light," he replied with an unspoken understanding between us.

The principal was not amused with Liam's foray into his toilet, nor with a couple of events during my teaching and coaching of sport at the school. When a boy brought one of his father's golf club and ball to class one day for show and tell I saw an opportunity for some interesting learning so took the class outside to give them a quick lesson on swinging a golf club and talk about it with them. The club was a nine iron and I thought I had plenty of space to chip the ball and keep it within the school grounds, but I was wrong. My class and I watched helplessly as the ball landed on the road in front of the school, bounced up and onto a low brick wall in front of a house opposite the school. Watching in silence, we all cringed as it shattered the big front window.

I coached the senior (boys) cricket team that won the local interschool competition. Only a few months after smashing the house window with a golf ball, I was working in the nets with them at lunchtime and felt like having a hit myself, so I asked one of the Year Six boys to bowl a few balls to me.

"Bobby, let's see how I go. See if you can bowl me out."

"Can I bowl fast, Mr Light?"

"The faster the better, Bobby"

I blocked the first couple of balls he bowled and then went for the next couple. On the last ball I hit the sweet spot and it felt great off the bat. The boys and I watched it climb much higher than I had intended to shatter the principal's window. There was absolute silence in the nets, and I could hear movement in the principal's office. All the boys and I stared at the shattered window until the principal stuck his head out the broken window that he carefully opened, with the ball in his hand: "Who did this?" he shouted.

"Mr Light, Sir," a student replied as they all looked at me.

Another bill from the glazier for the school, I thought.

In the second half of my first year at the new school, I was enjoying teaching but had not forgotten my dream of getting my black belt in Hong Kong. Neither Dave or Dick were anywhere near being able to go, but I was determined to. The problem was that I didn't know how to organise the trip until I talked to a mate of mine from Avalon who was an experienced traveller. Planning a surfing trip to Sri Lanka via Malaysia and Thailand at around the same time, I was hoping to go to Hong Kong. Ian was happy for me to join him and helped me organise my travels. I would travel with him to Malaysia and Thailand but from there I would head east to Hong Kong to train in karate, and he would head west to surf in Sri Lanka.

Leaving Australia to travel though Asia would be difficult to organise. The easy talk over the kitchen table at the Colo Valley farmhouse was behind me, and it was now time for action, but what did I know about international travel or Asia? Not much. At times I thought about the wisdom of quitting a secure job with a future to chase a dream. I had finally found a secure job that I enjoyed and was good at. My parents were proud of me and very happy that I seemed to be maturing ,but the timing and the opportunity I thought my idea offered meant I had to give it a go.

Finally, there I was, checking in at Sydney Airport and about to embark on the biggest adventure in my life. After check-in, I had a coffee, something to eat at one of the airport cafes, and talked with Ian about Asia.

I pushed through the thick wall of heat at Kuala Lumpur (KL) International Airport as I exited the plane and walked down the aluminium steps to the baking tarmac. Lined up at immigration I did a mental check. Passport? yes; tickets? yes; wallet? yes; cash and cash belt? yes. I had communicated by post with Cheuk Fai when he was living in Hong Kong and planned to train with him there, but now he would not be there when I arrived because he was moving to Sydney. It was poor planning, but he did connect me with karate friends of his in Kuala Lumpur and arrange for me to stay and train in Hong Kong with his older brother, Cheuk Sam. Ian and I stayed with the family of one of Cheuk Fai's friends in KL and trained in his *dojo* for a week.

KL was polluted and chaotic for me but had its own sense of order that became more evident as I settled in. Ian and I trained in a karate club and watched a couple of kung fu classes. He had never done any martial arts before but bought a karate *gi* so he could train with me because he thought it was a good opportunity. During the day, we walked around the city, taking in the feel of the place and its smells that included the stench of the fruit, durian. It tastes good but has been described as smelling like turpentine and onion, garnished with a gym sock. Or like rotten meat.

Everything was baffling and fascinating for me. I wrote and posted letters and post cards home to my family every few days for the first week to share the daily adventures I had had. At the beginning of each day, I looked forward to all the weird things we would see, smell, do or eat that day. My senses were all on full alert, and I was experiencing more than enough adventure.

After a week in KL, we moved up to Penang for more of the same heat, humidity, hard training, sweating, eating spicy local food, and drinking Tiger beer. The city hummed with small motor bikes that seemed to ignore any road rules there might have been. Ian and I hired one each for transport over the week we were there and rode out of the city to watch a local motorbike race with packs of locals on their bikes.

With hundreds of riders pumped up by the races, the trip back into the city turned into an unofficial race that was chaotic and dangerous, but so much fun. The bike riders formed packs on the way back to the city that I would enter from behind and work my way through to the front of. When there was a break in traffic coming from the opposite direction, I would then accelerate past as many cars as I could, with the next pack in my sights.

In Penang, Ian and I did more karate training but also frequented places where we could pay to enjoy the company of attractive young local women upstairs. It was all new for me, and the whole experience felt surreal. The only time I had ever been with a prostitute before this was on my 18th birthday in Sydney, where I picked up a street worker on William Street who walked me back to a dark, nearby house. A man was watching TV on the ground floor when we walked in and then upstairs and into a sad, dark bedroom.

"Come on, hurry up, love," she said.

I had an idea of what I might be in for before we arrived in Bangkok where it was also hot and humid but with different smells, food, and energy to Malaysia. It seemed more crowded and chaotic than Penang and KL.

We booked into a cheap hotel in the middle a notorious red-light district and were soon out on the street soaking up the atmosphere. It was a dream-like experience, and I didn't need any drugs to get high among the flashing, flickering neon lights, the thick heat, and the intense energy. I couldn't take my eyes off the hordes of exotically beautiful, brown skinned girls, and the way they looked at me as they flaunted themselves outside the go-go bars.

Just being in south-east Asia was totally different to anything I had experienced before, but this was at another level. It was like one big party with everybody looking to get laid. I had no idea places like this existed and posted many letters to my mates back home. I also regularly posted letters to my family in Byron Bay with many intricate drawings.

I was advised by friends who had been to these red-light areas in Asia to move around the many go-go bars and meet lots of girls before selecting one. It seemed like good advice, but I didn't follow it. The first place we entered had the usual dim lights and buzzing music that takes or keeps you out of touch with reality. We were ushered to a semi-private area for a few drinks and conversations with girls to decide who we would like to go with. After a hot bath and shower with one girl who captivated me, she gave me a long, sensual massage, and then sex. Driven by a combination of sexual desire and romanticism, I paid for her company for a week.

I felt my companion was special, and over the first couple of days even felt like I might have been falling in love with her enough to think about how I could come back to Bangkok, rescue her, and take her back to Australia. As an experienced traveller, Ian played the field and was free during the day. He accompanied my companion and me to the airport when I flew out to Hong Kong because my flight left the day before his. I felt a little lonely as we parted company from my escort but next time I met Ian back in Australia, he told me that she tried to score with him as soon as they got in the taxi on the way back to the hotel. It was her job.

Having spent more money in Bangkok than I budgeted for, I

arrived in Hong Kong with little cash to live on. Cheuk Fai was not there as he had moved to Sydney while I was making my way over, which was poor organisation on my part but his older brother, Chan Cheuk Sam kindly welcomed me into his Wan Chai home and traditional Chinese healing clinic.

"Oh, Ric Light! Welcome to Hong Kong."

"Thank you, Cheuk Sam, for letting me stay with you. It's been a long trip, but I am finally here. I'm looking forward to training with you."

"Come in, please," he said and then shouted something to his wife in Cantonese as he gestured to me.

The space inside Cheuk Sam's home and clinic was small, but it was big enough to train every day, and, when I needed to get outside, I went for a walk to explore Wan Chai. When planning my trip in Australia, I had seen photos in a surfing magazine (*Tracks*) of nice waves on Lantau Island and of the Po Lin Monastery where you could stay and eat vegetarian food. I thought I could take the odd break from karate training to catch a few waves and chill out in the Buddhist monastery where I would meditate. Unfortunately for me, the photos I had seen in *Tracks* were taken before or just after a typhoon and there were normally no waves. I carried my board around Asia for three months, but never put it in the water. Even the idea of staying at the monastery remained a dream as I did not have the money or time.

I slept on one of those plastic fold up beds you see poolside at cheap hotels, in the same room as the punching bag. I trained in Cheuk Sam's karate classes at night and during the day, hit and kicked the bag, and practised kata. I ate my main meals with him and his family and could only afford one cup of coffee at a local café each day and a copy of a very thin newspaper published in English.

I enjoyed training in Cheuk Sam's karate class and was confident sparring with his students but when the time for my grading test came, I was anxious. So much of my plan depended upon being awarded a blackbelt, and I had quit my job as a teacher to do it. I completed my *kihon* (basics) and felt that I did well enough but was worried about my *kata* (set forms) which came next. My grading finished with *kumite* (sparring) and I had no problem with a couple of Cheuk Sam's senior students but had to finish off by sparring with him and Cheuk Wah who was the brother between Cheuk

Fai and Cheuk Sam. I took a bit of a pounding from both of them, but I felt I did well enough and was reasonably confident that I'd passed but, at the end of the grading nobody said anything or even hinted at whether or not I had passed. I had booked my flight home to Sydney to depart three days after my grading and was beginning to feel anxious.

"Oh, Ric Light, you passed," Cheuk Sam said casually on my last day in Hong Kong.

"Really? You mean, I can wear a black belt?"

"Yes, you can. Well done; but work on your kata."

On the flight home, my mind drifted back to my early days in the Windsor boat shed with a weak leg, and the beginning of my determination to get my black belt. The plane landed in Sydney, and I spent the next two days there so that I could train at the main *dojo* for the karate style I was doing. I had been advised by a couple of my *sensei* that black belt was only the beginning of learning karate, and I believed them, but when I put my new blackbelt on for the first time before training at the main *dojo*, I was bursting with pride. The next day, I flew up to Byron Bay to set up a karate club that would allow me to achieve my goal of running a *dojo* in Byron Bay.

Back home in McGettigan's Lane, we chatted over a cup of tea and some of Mum's home-made biscuits on the veranda, and I couldn't wait to tell the story of my trip to Asia, my grading and my plans for the immediate future in Byron Bay. Over the next week Sue took a photo of me in my karate *gi* at The Pass for a story in *The Byron News* about me getting my black belt in Hong Kong and coming back to the Bay to start karate classes. I also put a small advertisement in the paper and hoped that at least a handful of people would turn up on the first night. With no martial arts schools in town, I was not sure how much interest there would be in karate.

After arriving at the scout hall very early on a Tuesday night I did some stretching, practised the *kata* I would teach and ran over in my head what I would do for my first class. Half an hour before the class was due to start, it was very quiet with only the odd car going past the hall. I heard distant conversation as what sounded like two people approached the door.

Two local boys I knew walked in the door and stopped in silence when they saw me. "Lighty, wow, look at you, mate!" one of them said. "Read about you in the paper and thought we'd come along to have a look. You're a black belt in karate! Cool."

People then began walking in, until there were more than 20 wanting to train with me. After putting my new students in lines, I stood in front of them in my *gi* with my black belt proudly tied around my waist.

The energy built as the class progressed, and my students developed an understanding of how it worked and the moves that I was asking them to do. At the end of the class, I took them through some meditation and felt the mellow, settled vibe as they left the hall. I was surprised at how well the class went and how comfortable I was teaching.

On the Thursday night, over 30 students signed the attendance book and two weeks after my first class I had fifty students training each week. What I lacked in experience I made up for with energy and enthusiasm. I delivered physically demanding classes that were a big hit with all the students. A good dose of discipline, lots of push-ups, expectation of effort, courage, respect, and a touch of humour were all well received.

A Taste for Challenges

I ran the first annual karate camp by the ocean and not far from the Queensland border. Each day, we jogged a kilometre up the long beach for each of the three training sessions after which we jogged back to camp for a very basic meal relax a little. We'd then jog back up the beach for the next session that typically went for one and a half to two hours. Training in the soft white sand, under an endless blue sky and a fierce sun, was tiring, but inspiring, with many students swimming in the surf between sessions and at the end of the day.

Fairlie was a strikingly beautiful women and a good athlete who was totally committed to karate and showed great promise from the first night she trained. From that first class, I also felt a strong sexual attraction between us. I tried to keep an emotional distance from her, but the constant interaction and the sense of being removed from the restraints of normal life made that difficult.

From the start of the camp on Friday afternoon, the eye contact between us increased in frequency and intensity with relaxed conversations between classes and over meals strengthening the connection between us. I don't know how obvious it was to the other students, but by the evening meal on Saturday night I knew where it was heading. That night, we had sex in her tent which made the sexual attraction between us difficult to hide throughout the next day at the camp and during classes back in Byron Bay.

I committed myself to emotional separation from her in class, but it was difficult, and this long affair ended badly for me. Years later, she left her American husband, running off with a younger American. As it happened, her husband had been importing huge amounts of marijuana by having it brought by boat from overseas.

I ran most of the karate camps after the first one up in the hills around Minyon Falls in the hinterlands. We slept in tents in the bush under a star-filled, black sky and began each day with a morning run through narrow winding tracks. Food was very basic with no meat or dairy, wholegrain rice, very basic vegetables like beans, soy sauce and black tea. A designated crew cooked a hot dinner with leftovers eaten cold for breakfast with something else added and the same for lunch. The hot drink was black billy tea, and there was no smoking (anything).

Removed from the day-to-day routines of our normal lives, we were totally immersed in a world of karate, but, by Sunday, most students were exhausted and riding on the energy we had produced. The meat eaters were starving as they packed and cleaned up late Sunday afternoon, and the energy that we had created as a group was dissipating. Most of the students were tired, sore, and hungry but satisfied, and so was I. These spartan camps combined karate, teaching, and nature, as three important things for me. They also had a strong influence on my students' internal development, and mine.

Most of my students at the Mullumbimby *dojo* lived in the hills out the back of Mullumbimby, with more than half the class being what I called hippies. There were five or six of these students training with me two nights a week, and they were very good. They all had karate *gi* that they did not seem to wash much and stunk of garlic when they started sweating because they chewed on raw garlic during the day for health reasons. They had been training out in the hills with Jack Roberts (pseudonym) who had fled city life for an alternative lifestyle structured around karate. As numbers increased in all my clubs, I asked Jack to teach for me in the Mullumbimby *dojo,* and he agreed, but he was too tough on most students. Within about a month, numbers had fallen off, with only the core of his original students remaining. I drove over to the club to speak with him after his class.

"Jack, first I want to thank you for taking these classes."

"No problem."

"The trouble for me is that class numbers have dropped down to just a few students. This makes it difficult to pay the hall rent and pay you for teaching. It's important to keep the number of students training or build them if possible. I think you have been too hard on them."

"I'm just training like I always do."

"Yes, I understand that, but it does not suit most people. I'm sorry, but I will take the classes myself again from next week to build them back to the numbers we had before. Hope that is not too much of a problem for you."

"That's okay. I teach karate like I think it should be taught. It's your call."

"I know that, Jack. And I appreciate your commitment, but I will teach the classes from next week."

After our discussion, he did not say much, but I felt tension between us. We had very different perspectives on karate and were very different people.

Every year, I had an annual interclub championship in the Byron Bay Literary Institute where some students in the three clubs met each other for the first time. Tyler (pseudonym) had only one leg from the knee down but trained as hard as anyone else did in the Lismore club. With his *gi* on, and his artificial leg attached, his handicap was hidden, and he made it through to the second round. His opponent in the second round had never met him and didn't know Tyler had an artificial leg.

For most students, the interclub tournament was the biggest karate event of the year and there was a lot of excitement in the air as students arrived, changed, and warmed up. One defensive move I taught some of my karate students came from Jin Wu Koon kung fu. Instead of blocking a front kick or moving to evade it, the defender would use a sweep and pull action. This involved sweeping the kick away while catching and pulling the heel of the opponent's kicking foot to shift the kicker's weight forward and put them off balance. When correctly executed, it would make them land on the front foot where the defender could score with a punch.

Tyler launched a strong mid-section front kick that his opponent defended against with a sweeping kung fu defence. As he swept to catch Tyler's foot and pull him forward, he ripped his artificial leg off. There was absolute silence in the hall, with all eyes on Tyler's lower leg lying two metres away from him on the old timber floor after half a rotation. Tyler's opponent stood in amazement, shifting his gaze from Tyler, standing on one leg to the artificial leg he had just ripped off, back to Tyler, and then to me. *Yame* (stop) I called, and the two opponents returned to their marks where they had started, with Tyler hopping on one leg.

"Go and get your leg, Tyler," I told him quietly.

"Oooosssu!" he replied with a cursory bow and then hopped over to it to attach it and walk back to his mark and assume his ready stance.

"*Hajime!*" I commanded in a strong voice to continue the bout.

My earlier exposure to self-hypnosis and tapping into my capabilities shaped my personal development, and my teaching in Byron Bay. Over my first few years of karate in Sydney, the head of the organisation who I will call Robert, brought the young boy who lived next door to a class to demonstrate self-hypnosis. I watched him insert a long hypodermic needle through the webbing between his finger and thumb with no bleeding or apparent pain. I was hugely impressed and jumped at the opportunity to learn how to do this by doing a course of study with Robert. I picked it up so well that Robert invited me to do public demonstrations of 'mind control' for him.

When I first saw the demonstration of mind control, I didn't think I could do it but, after my course with him, I could. I grew in confidence and took on more challenges. At demonstrations in Sydney, I pushed needles through the skin on my chest, and cheek. Then I moved on to pushing a hypodermic needle in through my right cheek and mouth then out through my left cheek. I surprised myself with how I could go within myself to relax, ground myself and *know* that it would not hurt.

I learned how much more I could do than what I thought I could. After being amazed at what someone else could do, I was soon able to do it myself and take it further. The keys to doing this for me were deep relaxation, self-awareness, visualisation, and self-belief. I then took it up a notch by lying on a bed of long, sharp nails that one of my students in Byron Bay who was a carpenter had made. I did this to promote my martial arts business at martial arts demonstrations and packed kickboxing nights where it was televised a few times. Once I learned to accept and control pain, lying on a bed of nails was not difficult.

The first time I lay on the bed of nails in public, I needed about thirty seconds to slow my heart rate down and tune into my body. I visualised myself doing it then took ten seconds or so to go deep inside myself and snap into a state of catalepsy. From a standing position, my whole body snapped into a rigid, arched shape that two of my students carried like a surfboard with one holding my heels and another holding my shoulders to lay me on the bed of nails. I focussed on my body, my being, and my spirit, with little awareness of what was happening outside. I felt the long, sharp nails against my skin but no pain. I knew they could not hurt me. Once I relaxed, I shifted some of my awareness from being completely internal to what was happening outside.

Lying on the bed of nails, I had several slabs of concrete placed on my abdomen to be smashed with a sledgehammer. In preparation for this I stayed relaxed and tightened only my abdominal muscles at the precise moment of impact while staying relaxed on the bed of nails.

Once I had mastered the bed of nails, I needed a new challenge that would impress an audience. For this I lay between two beds of nails with one pointing up and the top one pointing down as a bed-of-nails-sandwich, with me in the middle. My brother Greg would go into catalepsy then have two of my students lay him of the top bed of nails and have the concrete slabs placed on his abdomen to be smashed with a sledgehammer. I was totally focused on what I was doing and never felt pain or discomfort. To share what I had learned, I started my own classes in mind control that I conducted at my parents' house in McGettigan's Lane with some good results.

I enjoyed being able to help people achieve things that they didn't think they could while exploring my ability to assist healing and achieving goals that they through were beyond them. In his mid-twenties, Graham was intellectually and physically affected after a childhood car accident and could only walk with the use of a walking stick. Greg and I sometimes had coffee with him at a café in the old Jonson Street dive shop and one day I suggested he join a group about to do mind control with me, and he did. His ability to become one in mind and body and focus everything on one task was so impressive that it was almost scary at times. In one activity, I used a representation of a spiral that I would ask people to look deeply into and feel it pulling them in and pushing them out. When I did this with Graham, his body became rigid, and he seemed to defy gravity as he leaned in toward the spiral and away from it. It was as though he was being controlled by some mysterious force.

After six weeks of classes, Graham didn't need his walking stick and joined my karate classes but had to stand at the back of the class because he could not move as well as the others and often fell over. When he went down, it took a lot of effort for him to get back up on his feet. I would tell the class to stop and keep their eyes to the front of the *dojo* then walk over to him and quietly tell him to get up. Sometimes, I would help him a little, but most of the time I would not.

"Get up Graham—on your own." I said quietly, as he looked up at me. "You know you can do it."

"You're a bastard, Lighty," he mumbled under his breath as he made his way up to a standing position and back into his karate stance with a half-smile on his face.

I enjoyed competing in karate tournaments and was good enough to be selected in a couple of state and national teams but questioned my ability to fight for real. Most of the karate I did was geared toward tournaments with rules developed to test skill while eliminating the risk of injury. There were some tough men competing in these tournaments, but I had doubts about how effective the technique used would be in a real fight which led to an interest in kickboxing.

In Australia, I fought under rules that did not allow kicks to the opponent's legs and favoured boxers wanting to fight in kickboxing tournaments. Allowing heavy kicks to the thighs makes it a very different fight. As well as fighting in Queensland, NSW and Victoria, I had a few fights in Asia under rules much like Muay Thai.

In 1979, I was invited by Cheuk Fai to compete in an international full contact kung fu tournament, staged in the middle of a Kuala Lumpur football field. From the time we landed in KL, I was excited but didn't really know what the rules were until the day before my fight. The lack of an interpreter during discussions with officials led me to wrongly believe that groin kicks and head butts were allowed but mouthguards weren't. "Are you sure"? I asked. The official smiled and nodded affirmatively but, had actually been trying to convey to me that biting was not allowed. The rules were similar to Muay Thai (Thai boxing) but we fought in a ring with no ropes.

I had calmed myself before the fight but, as soon as I stepped onto the stage in front of a huge crowd, I was unsettled and anxious. My opponent stared fiercely into my eyes as the referee explained the rules. I was a mess of emotions that I dealt with by going in hard as soon as the referee started the fight. Early in the fight, we clashed and did some ugly grappling until the referee separated us. Near the edge of the ring, I hit my opponent with a strong mid-section front kick that propelled him into the audience. He made his way back onto the stage and, as soon as the referee called for us to re-engage, he charged at me. I felt my front kick sink into his solar plexus and he dropped to the floor, gasping for his first few breaths of air and was counted out as he crawled back to his corner. I had won my first fight.

I made the semi-final in my weight division where I took a nasty (illegal) kick in the groin that was so painful I could not continue. Groin kicks were against the rules but my opponent was not disqualified and I was eliminated. I had watched the fighter who I should have faced in the final and had been preparing myself for the fight of my career so was very disappointed not to be in the ring for the final. I was even more disappointed when my opponent from the semi-final that made it to the final by kicking me in the groin showed no courage and seemed happy with second before the fight even started. I was not sure I could have won but would have given it 100 percent and thought that maybe I should have pushed through the pain when kicked in the groin.

Two years later, I was part of another team of Jin Wu Koon fighters who competed in a big Hong Kong, New Year's Eve tournament. Using rules very similar to Mui Thai, it was run like a boxing tournament with fighters from different countries matched for the one fight contested over three rounds. I was matched with the Malaysian champion in my weight division and had to shape up to him at a promotional event for the Hong Kong press. I felt like I was in a movie, and I might have been.

When I was getting changed for my fight and on my own, I heard a lot of excited talk in Cantonese and things being dragged, pushed, and carried toward me. I turned to see a Hong Kong movie star walking around the corner and toward me, followed by cameras, bright lights and a crowd of people speaking excitedly. He moved toward me to open one of the lockers that was about ten metres away from me and repeated this a few times before moving off and leaving me. I later found out that they were getting some footage of the real thing for a movie.

After the actors and film crew left the locker room, I had plenty of time to prepare myself for entry into a world where violence is not only allowed but rewarded. My fight plan was simple. I would hammer my opponent's legs to soften him early, move him into a corner and get in close to attack with punches, knees, and elbows.

As I faced my opponent in the middle of the ring, nervousness gave way to a focus on the task in front of me and wanting to get on with it. The referee sent us to our corners then called us back to start the fight. After a few early clashes, I settled enough to think and look for opportunities as we both engaged in more thoughtful tactics. Late in the first round, I hit him in the face with an elbow strike that stunned him and sent him staggering back a couple of steps. On the referee's instruction, I went back to my corner where I waited for him to restart the fight, but he stopped it. He then called me into the centre of the ring to hold my gloved hand up in the air.

The Jin Wu Koon fighters did well. When it was finished, we all enjoyed a few drinks and great Chinese food. The others could all relax after that, but I had a karate grading for my second dan black belt a week after the tournament.

In 1977, Chan Cheuk Sam graded me to *shodan* (1st dan) in Hong Kong and wanting to make the most of being there again I asked to be graded for *nidan* (2nd dan), four years after my *shodan* (2nd dan) grading.

Greg stayed in Hong Kong because we were going to spend a week together in the Philippines on the way home and came to my grading. Six of us walked through dimly lit streets toward where I would be graded by the two Chan brothers. I engaged in conversation with Cheuk Sam, but this faded out as we seemed to be approaching our destination. Walking in silence from that point on, the mood changed, and I sensed it was going to be a tough grading.

My grading was conducted in what seemed like the empty first floor of a house with concrete walls, a tiled floor, and windows with steel bars. It was a cold and hard physical environment that seemed to suit what I thought I was in for. After completing my *kihon* (basics) and *kata* (forms), it was time for *kumite*. The sparring with Cheuk Wah was intense, but I was doing well enough until he kicked me in the groin. It was not intentional but none-the-less painful, and they gave me five minutes to recover. It was then time for me to take on Cheuk Sam, 'the bulldozer'. It was a tough encounter with both of us being driven backwards into a concrete wall a couple of times. I felt like we were the only two people in the room and in the heat of the battle struck Cheuk Sam with an elbow in the face. The rules were moderate body contact and no contact to the head, but I had elbowed my *sensei* in the face. I stood facing Chan Cheuk Sam with his bottom lip split and Cheuk Wah attempting to stem the blood seeping from it. Sweating, with my heart pumping in my ears, I regretted what I had done.

He raised his head and glaring at me, said: "I said no contact. You do that again, and I will kill you!"

I apologised but knew he was going to come at me hard and was unsure how to respond. A week earlier I had been fighting with no limitations on contact and would have been rewarded for the blow I just delivered, but this was a very different situation. I regretted striking him in the face with my elbow because it was disrespectful and because of the situation it put me in. I knew he was going to get even with me, but I could not risk striking him in the head again, so decided to adopt a defensive mind set. Cheuk Wah brought us both back to where we started and reminded me that there was no contact to the head, then told us to start. We clashed again and Cheuk Sam struck me in the face with his shoulder. The impact slammed me back against the hard wall that I slid down. Sitting on the cold, tiled floor, and only semi-conscious, I was numb in the face as blood poured from my shattered nose over my white *gi*.

"Get up, Ric Light, get up!" Cheuk Sam shouted, standing above me.

Cheuk Wah calmed him down in Cantonese and asked me if I was okay. I was dazed with my nose pushed across to the left of my face but stood up and asked my sensei to straighten it, which he did but without a lot of care.

Stunned, Greg stood in silence during the grading but came up to me when it had finished to check on me. "You okay, Ric? Do you need anything?"

The next day, Cheuk Sam told me I had passed.

My participation in kickboxing tournaments encouraged me to promote them on the far north coast of NSW and the Gold Coast in Queensland. Planning in the promotion of a big kickboxing event on the Gold Coast, I wanted the top karate student from *Sensei* Brian Ellison's *dojo* to compete in the main event. I wanted him to fight one of Cheuk Fai's best kickboxers, so I drove up to ask him face to face. Brian was one of the toughest martial artists I had ever sparred with and had always helped me when I asked. He regularly refereed for me at karate tournaments so thought I'd ask him but face to face.

"G'day, Ric," he said as he opened the door

"Hi Brian. I have a proposal I drove up to talk to you about…"

"We can talk inside," he said and gestured for me to come in.

He asked me to sit down at the dining table, sat down himself and immediately rolled a joint. After lighting it and with nothing said, he handed it to me. It was very strong, and I soon found myself staring at the deadly Japanese weapons hanging on the main wall in the room and spacing out from time to time as we shared the joint. The silence was broken when he snatched a fly in flight and threw it in the fish tank where it was instantly devoured by a carnivorous fish.

"I have an idea for a big kickboxing tournament on the Gold Coast that I need your help with," I said as I handed him the written proposal.

I began to explain how I would like his top student to compete in the main bout, but he gestured with his hand for me to stop talking without looking up. After a minute or so he put down the paper, nodded and pushed it toward me.

"We're in," he said.

Punching with bare fists and boxing gloves requires very different technique so I offered to lend him some boxing gloves for his student to practise with. He said they didn't need to practise with gloves. His student would not do any special preparation and would fight like they always did. On the night I refereed the main bout, and with Brian's student covered in his own blood, I had to stop the fight. Brian was not happy but accepted it.

At kickboxing events, I always provided entertainment, which often included me lying on a bed of nails and having a stack of concrete slabs smashed on my abdomen or doing the bed of nails sandwich. For the Gold Coast event, I decided to do something different by hiring a local stripper but asked her to leave her tiny

G-string on. This was certainly commercialising martial arts, but I believed that kickboxing and traditional Japanese martial arts, like karate, were totally different. And it *was* the Gold Coast.

I supplemented my income from martial arts with casual teaching and mostly in PE, which also allowed me to keep in contact with teaching. On a rainy day at a high school in Lismore, two teachers and I had to entertain our male students with sport videos because we had no available inside space. I thought they might enjoy a video of the Gold Coast kickboxing night so put it on and sat up the back of the room chatting to the other two teachers.

When the room suddenly fell quiet, I looked up to see the stripper halfway through her act on the video. I pushed my way through the mass of boys sitting in front of me with eyes glued to the screen and turned off the video, but not before she exposed her breasts. "Ooohhhh Sirrr!" was the collective response as the screen went black.

My life in Byron Bay over the late seventies and early eighties was dominated by martial arts, but I did pursue some other interests and challenges. In the early seventies, my parents bought an old house and an acre of land in McGettigan's Lane from an American who had moved to Byron Bay. He was a prominent social figure at the time among the wave of newcomers attracted to the Bay over that period.

At one of his big parties, everybody was stoned, and the kitchen was packed with people who had the munchies. With the music loud and the air thick with the pungent odour of *ganja*, I stood shoulder to shoulder in a crowd inching toward the kitchen bench. I was almost salivating as I finally began to make myself a peanut butter sandwich and could taste it before putting it in my mouth when someone gave me a solid nudge from the side:

"Would you mind making one for me mate?" he asked.

"Haven't you got any arms?" I replied facetiously.

His reply of "No, I haven't" shocked me when I saw that he didn't.

He was a local guy who was born without arms as a thalidomide victim and was renowned for driving a truck using his feet. I apologised profusely, offered him my slice and asked him how many more he wanted. He laughed and all was good.

In 1966, at the first dinner in our Lighthouse Road home, Sue asked our parents to buy her a horse. She was only six at the time so had to wait, but a few years but later they bought her a young, black, and wilful gelding. She taught herself to ride on the beach where she cantered and sometimes galloped on Shiloh down to Main Beach and back.

The house my parents bought in McGettigan's Lane had been occupied by squatters and Bill thought about knocking it down, but decided to renovate it and bought an extra four acres. Built in the 1890s, our new home had originally been the home of Bernard and Margaret McGettigan with McGettigan's Lane made to provide access to it. Six kilometres from town on five acres we lived a very different lifestyle, and it was good for Sue's horse Shiloh. He had a lot more room than the paddock in town and lots of space for long rides around Ewingsdale which was good timing for him because Sue was losing interest in him.

I hadn't been on a horse since Impedance tossed be over the fence but decided to look after Shiloh and teach myself to ride. I started on our property and then rode him at a walking pace up and down the lane with very few cars to scare him. Despite him being a very smart and strong-willed horse, my slow walks down the lane and back were trouble free.

Smithy was very involved with horses and lived down the lane toward the cattle dip. Standing in front of his house as I rode past on Shiloh one day, he stopped me:

"G'day. How ya goin?"

"Good, thanks," I replied as I stopped, and he approached me.

"I'm Keith…"

"I'm Ric. Nice to meet you."

"How long you been riding?"

"Not so long but getting there."

"Wondering if you'd be interested in playing polocrosse? We need one more rider for our team. Reckon you'd be interested?"

I didn't know what polocrosse was, but it sounded interesting after Smithy briefly explained it to me, so I turned up for practice the following week. As an inexperienced rider, it was very difficult for me to play, but I stuck at it for two years on top of my martial arts, surfing, rugby and casual teaching. I fell off a few times but did my best to hang on when Shiloh charged off the field and into the carpark. I enjoyed riding him into town, cross country, as a little adventure for me once a week. Over this long ride, I didn't see anyone until I hit town for a coffee at the Byronian Café, next to Railway Park. I would give Shiloh some water, read the paper, and then ride home.

After the family moved to McGettigan's Lane, I developed a connection with Ewingsdale that became stronger, year by year. My connection with nature there included consuming the magic mushrooms (gold tops) that grew around our property. Greg and I, and our friends, knew they were dangerous because it was so difficult to know how strong they were, and we had heard of some people losing their minds. Probably the biggest problem with magic mushies was their hideous taste and how revoltingly slimy they were when we tried to eat them raw and straight out of the ground. Greg and I solved this problem by boiling them and using the water to make strong coffee that we would share with friends in the humpy. Deeply involved in talking, playing guitar and singing, we would forget about the gold top coffee we'd drunk until it began to take effect. One by one, we would all feel the trip begin and couldn't play guitar anymore. Usually we would not physically go very far but the mental and spiritual experience was always mind blowing, as was being totally immersed in the smallest of objects, and particularly objects of nature like leaves, twigs, flowers and even a blade of grass. The privacy down around the back of the property before any development allowed us all to behave like idiots without being seen or heard.

Every Christmas, the Light family shared one double length joint over dinner on the veranda, as the only time Mum ever smoked *ganja*. Bill had stopped smoking tobacco so really enjoyed having a joint in his hand and had to be constantly reminded not to Bogart (hog) the joint. Over this period, Betty became a mother figure to many of my friends and students who were originally from out of town. She was known for her tea, bikkies, and chats on the veranda among my friends and karate students. She was happy to just listen, be empathetic and offer support with a nod her head and a soft murmuring like "Oh, I understand," "I see," or "You'll be alright."

On one of my martial arts visits to Hong Kong, I saw how

people made the most of the little space available to them and I had to keep the build of my studio to a tight budget. I built a high-pitched roof and put in an elevated bed with a ladder that I had to climb up to get to my bed. The bed was about 180cm above the floor with a little sofa under it and was a quirky feature of the house.

The Assassin Calls

I awoke to the slow squeak of the French doors opening but heard no footsteps. Sensing someone in the dark room below me, I cautiously sat up, and listened but heard nothing.

"Ric Light?" I heard after a few seconds of silence, and I knew who it was.

"Jack, what are you doing here?" I asked as I angled the bedside reading lamp down toward him and switched it on. Wearing a black *gi* and soft black slippers, he shifted uncomfortably under the light of the lamp and spoke without pausing about heroin dealers and paedophiles in black plastic rooms up in the hinterland. He wasn't making much sense, so I interrupted him.

"What's that got to do with me?"

"I want to know where you stand," he replied as he tried to look me in the eyes but looked away because of the lamp focused on him.

Eighteen months earlier, he approached me in a bar to talk about smack (heroin) dealers who were hiding in the hinterland. He wanted to do something about them and was after assurance from me that if he got in trouble with them I would back him up. I told him not to go looking for trouble, assuming that I would back him up. Increasingly agitated in my room and not making much sense to me, he spoke about negative interactions between us: about me cutting him at a camp the only time we ever sparred and him not being able to continue because Cheuk Fai stopped him, and how I cancelled his teaching at the Mullumbimby dojo. During a tirade that was building in intensity and anger, I interrupted him to say, "Jack, everything's not black and white."

"Yes, it fuckin' is!" he shouted back, giving my kitchen draws a thumping front kick that knocked a teacup into the sink, and smashed it.

I knew him as an intense man for who karate was his life, but there was something very wrong with him. After about twenty minutes of monologue, he suddenly stopped talking, turned, and walked out without saying anything more. I heard him crunch through the leaves and bush outside my house and five minutes later, a car started in the distance and drove off down the Lane. It was an intense twenty minutes that did not make much sense to me, and the room was full of bad energy as I lay in silence, and eventually fell asleep. In the morning, I went up to my parents' house and told Betty what had happened, over a cup of tea on the veranda.

"Oh, that is very odd," she said. "It's really a bit creepy him coming into your place at that time of night in his black clothes and raving on like that."

Later, I repeated my account of Jack's visit to Bill who agreed that it was very strange and suggested that "He was probably on some strong drugs, Ric."

The following morning, when we saw the front page of the *Northern Star*, with a photo of him being arrested, I realised how close I had come to a violent death that night.

According to the newspaper and the local television news, Jack believed he had been a samurai in a previous life and that a girl working at The Popular Café in Mullumbimby had been his lover. Believing that Ric Light and some of his black belts had captured her and taken her to Byron Bay, he was going to kill them all and cut out her heart. Standing inside my studio, venting his frustration and anger, he had two bowie knives concealed under his black *gi* top that he was going to kill me with. The police searched his home in the hills after his arrest and found a pamphlet on Chinese techniques for killing an opponent with a knife. At his trial in Sydney, in which I was a witness, he explained how a strong dose of LSD had pushed him over the edge.

After leaving my studio, Jack drove back to Brunswick Heads then set off to run along the beach back toward Byron Bay. The distance along the beach from Brunswick to the Belongil Creek is about 10 kilometres and would have been another five to six kilometres to my place in McGettigan's Lane, which suggests he was confused and not functioning very well.

On his run, Jack became entangled in a fisherman's line. The fisherman abused Jack and an argument followed during which Jack stabbed him and told him to "walk into the sea and cleanse thy soul." Penetrating the fisherman's ribs, the knife pierced his heart.

Jack then ran back to Brunswick, where he banged on somebody's door looking for a car to drive home, covered in the fisherman's blood. He was later arrested while riding a horse up in the hills at the end of what must have been a long and chaotic day.

Unsettled by this bizarre incident and wanting some answers, I visited Jack in Grafton gaol. It was my first time in a goal and a little unsettling. I had been thinking about what I would say to him and ask him during the drive from Byron Bay to Grafton but forgot it all when I sat down facing him. The conversation began awkwardly with a few pauses:

"G'day Jack."

"G'day Ric."

"What happened, Jack? And why?"

"Ric, I was totally off my face and fucked up. I don't have anything against you, honestly, and am sorry for what happened. I don't know what happened that night or why."

"I know we've had a few differences of opinion and have a different view of karate but why did you come to my home that night with those knives"?

"I went on a binge. I just lost it."

He explained how he had taken too much very strong LSD after taking other drugs over the few days leading up to that night. He assured me again that he had nothing against me and told me it was the LSD he had taken that caused him to do what he did. I also visited him in Long Bay gaol. Much later I spoke to someone I knew who had been in the same goal as Jack, at the same time. He told me that Jack spent his time inside training and pounding the walls of the prison with his fists at night, which earned him respect among other inmates. At his trial, he was found not guilty due to insanity and locked up at the Governor's pleasure, but later released. One of my Mullumbimby *dojo* students from up in the hills, had moved to Sydney to study law and helped him.

After the drama with Jack, Vanessa returned to Sydney, and I continued with my martial arts. I had worked my way up the rankings in kickboxing and when the reigning champion in my weight division retired, I was elevated to Australian champion, but I did not get a fight for a while and decided to retire myself. It had all suddenly lost its meaning for me, and I was beginning to feel that the big adventure of my life had stalled.

My decision to quit teaching, get a black belt in Hong Kong and pursue a martial arts business back home set me on a path that encouraged me to follow my passion. For eight years, I lived my dream and grew as a person but, by 1984, I felt my life had plateaued. My martial arts journey began in 1974 with me waiting on the deck outside the Windsor *dojo* for the *sensei* to come and open the door.

I had no idea what was involved in a karate class but was going to make a start. One person was already there waiting outside in his white *gi* and belt, then two more arrived wearing yellow belts. I wondered what sort of deadly attack they could unleash on me if I said the wrong thing so said very little. I felt physically inadequate but loved what we did in the first class, during which the boat shed was the *dojo*.

Every time I walked into the *dojo,* I entered a world of order, certainty, strong values and ethics, deep concentration and being in the moment. It quickly became a special place for me as I faced external and internal challenges and could feel myself changing. Despite my weak left leg and lack of flexibility, I threw myself into it and loved it. I loved the workout, the full exertion of punching and kicking and particularly when timed with a big *kiai.* My mind was racing as I drove home from Windsor after my first night of training.

I needed a change. I needed new direction but was not sure what it would be or how I could find it. I decided to leave my martial arts clubs in the hands of my senior students and move down to Sydney a year after Vanessa did.

Vanessa worked as a dental nurse in Manly and was flatting with a male friend of hers in Mona Vale when I moved in. I quickly put on my jeans to walk her outside early one morning and give her a goodbye kiss for the day. I did not bother to put a shirt on and braved the cold for what I thought would just be a few minutes. As soon as she drove off, I sprinted back toward the warmth of the apartment and a hot cup of tea, but the door was locked. I tried several times but could not open it. My house keys and wallet were inside, and I was locked out with no shoes or shirt on! I quickly checked all possibilities for getting inside through any open windows without success but did have the keys to my motorbike in the pocket of my jeans.

I called Vanessa from a public phone. "Ness, I'm locked out. The keys are inside, and I'm freezing with no shirt or shoes. Can you drive home and open the door?"

"I can't, Ric. I wish I could, but I just can't leave work. "

"Okay. I have my bike keys so I'll have to ride into Manly and pick up the keys from you. It's really cold, so please have them ready. I'll be blue when I walk in."

"I will. And be careful."

I rode 16 kilometres to Manly, wearing only a pair of jeans in the middle of winter, and I felt frozen to my bones. At first, I just felt very cold but gradually became numb with no shoes, shirt, gloves, or helmet and it seemed to take forever to get to Manly.

Shattering the warm quietness of the waiting room, I burst in and in a loud voice asked, "Ness, where are the keys?"

"There—in front of you" she said, pointing to them.

"Thanks, I gotta go. I am so cold I am numb," I mumbled as I picked the keys up and disappeared out the door.

She had to explain who I was, what was going on, and apologise to the waiting patients after I left the room.

Later, the three of us moved into an apartment near the Newport Arms pub. I did casual teaching and after a year picked up a contract to teach physical education at Balgowlah Boys' High School three days a week. I joined the Warringah Rats rugby club but lasted only two half seasons. I did a little training with Cheuk Fai from time to time, but Newport is a long way from Chinatown where his Jin Wu Koon club was.

The booming sport of triathlon gave me new direction in life. I started doing triathlons for fun but soon became hyper-competitive, spending too much money on expensive bikes, running shoes and equipment to give me an edge over my rivals. Vanessa also started competing but in a healthier way than I was, and we started travelling to races across NSW and in southeast Queensland.

I loved the excitement and energy I felt when being part of big, or even massive, triathlons. At the City of Sydney triathlon, I lined up, shoulder to shoulder on a wharf with a thousand other competitors to swim across the harbour to Blues Point. I was a good swimmer so made my way to the front of the competitors packed onto the wharf where I focused on the water, waiting until the start gun fired. I hit the water with a mass of other swimmers trying to get to the front of the pack in the white churning water and worked my way toward the front of the pack. What a blast it was! I was never a distance athlete but was a strong swimmer and cyclist who would usually get off my bike in the top ten percent of competitors. On the run, I didn't pass anybody and was always passed by competitors, ranging from young teenagers to old men and women on the run. Up until the run, I was focused on inching my way forward in the pack one by one, but, on the run, it was the opposite. I came to dread the patter of the next runner approaching me from behind and then passing me.

My involvement included organising the first two triathlons in Byron Bay over 1986 and 1987. I competed in the first one and thought I was going to come second until being run down by one of the local councillors not far from the finish. Triathlons appealed to my competitive nature and gave me something to commit to but consumed so much of my time, energy, and money that it cost me my relationship with Vanessa. Life in Sydney was initially interesting because it was different, but after Vanessa left me, I slowed down to engage in some much-needed reflection. I wasn't going anywhere. I wasn't discovering much more about myself, and everything I was doing just seemed like a distraction from the fact that I had lost my way.

Andrew was one of my former 'hippy' karate students at the Mullumbimby *dojo* who had moved to Sydney to complete a law degree at the University of NSW. Rudi was one of my karate and kung fu students who had completed a diploma and then a degree in sports science. Their success highlighted my loss of direction and encouraged me to think about my future and further education.

I graduated from Lismore Teachers College in 1973 and, later, studied off-campus to eventually get my three-year, Diploma in Teaching. Now back in Sydney, I thought that maybe I should get a degree, so I enrolled in a Bachelor of Education (Physical Education) which would qualify me to teach physical education in secondary schools.

At 32, I applied as a mature age student to get into an elite physical education program at Kuring-Gai College of Advanced Education (KCAE). I knew I would have to work hard to get through. It only accepted 25 students a year for the four-year physical education degree with five of these places offered to mature age students. KCAE offered me a place due to my teaching experience and sporting achievements with two years advanced standing which meant that I could complete the four-year degree in two years. It was exactly what I needed.

The intellectual stimulation of studying and the direction it provided were great for me, but financially it was killing me. I had classes every day so, unless I took a day off, I could only do casual school teaching between semesters, and outside school holidays. I picked up a job washing dishes at a French restaurant near the Newport Arms because I sometimes rode with the boss. It was only two minutes' walk from my apartment, but the work was awful. With no dishwasher, I had to wash all the greasy, buttery dishes, pots, pans, and cutlery in the one sink. The waiting staff would pile the dirty dishes and cutlery on my right. I would almost be finished when someone would dump another big pile of dirty dishes and I would have to start again. There were hours and hours of washing up and I was always last to finish. I had intellectual stimulation during the day but was brain dead at night.

I'd had worse jobs, but working as a dishwasher was getting me down. Low pay, little to no satisfaction and working until late at night. I had to find other work. There was a male student who was always beaming with confidence and fashionably, yet casually, dressed. Scott had model good looks and seemed to work out, but I thought he was a bit of a pretty boy. In conversation with a couple of female students at the college, one of them told me that he earned a lot of money as a dancer, so I asked him about it.

"I hate to be so direct, but I wanted to ask you about your work. Your work outside college."

"No problem, Ric. Fire away."

"I hear you work as a dancer and do pretty well out of it."

"Yeah, mate, I do work as a dancer and do okay with it."

"What type of dance?"

"Well, I'm a male stripper."

"Really?"

"Yes, really." he said laughing.

I was lost for words at first. I knew nothing about male stripping, but, after he told me how much he earned, I was interested.

"So, what do you do as a stripper? How do you become one?"

"Well, you take your clothes off in a way that entertains women. You need to be reasonably good looking, confident, and have a good body. You should be able to dance a bit and perform in front of crowds of women. Why do you ask? Are you interested?"

"Well, yes. I can't really dance, but I could use moves from martial arts. Would that work?"

"I think it could." He looked me up and down and added, "You look like you've got a good body and you're confident. The martial arts thing might work. Try it."

"How?"

"If you're interested, I can get you an audition at a big club, but you'll need a routine, music, and a costume. And a character."

Scott arranged an audition for me at a place called Jamison Street, which was the most famous venue for male stripping in Sydney. It could attract crowds of up to 500 screaming women packed in for a show. I designed my routine and costume and began practising at home in my little lounge room. I decided on my character as the ninja for the show with a routine in which I could use my martial arts skills. My costume was a black karate *gi* with Velcro strips on the seams to allow slowly peeling or dramatically ripping off sections. I had black gloves and black material wrapped around my head with only my eyes visible to start with. Scott helped me make a tape for my music with changes timed to match changes in my routine. He took me to Jamison Street before my audition to watch him perform and see what happens. It gave me a feel for the whole thing and the almost unreal environment I was going to perform in.

I watched Scott perform his routine and was impressed with how well he communicated with the mass of sometimes crazy women, and how much of a showman he was. The audience of around 300 erupted when he ripped off his pants to a dramatic change in the music and held his masculine pose for them to savour. I was inspired by his performance and the amazing atmosphere at Jamison Street. By this time in my life, I had overcome my shyness as a child to become a very confident person, and sometimes too confident. I was comfortable being the centre of attention, but, at Jamison Street, I would be facing a new challenge. Was I going to do something that could make me look and feel like a fool?

I fought in an international full contact kung fu tournament in Kuala Lumpur in front of 8000 spectators and a packed house of 3500 in Hong Kong's Queen Elizabeth stadium, but with around 250 rabid women at Jamison Street, it would be a different type of audience. It seemed very different to fighting in a ring but, in some ways, required similar mental preparation for me.

As my time to perform approached, I stretched and ran over my routine in my head for the last time as the previous act finished and the audience bayed for more. I felt apprehensive waiting off stage before being given the nod to get ready behind the drawn curtains. I settled myself by controlling my breathing and grounding myself to stay calm. Before the curtains opened, I assumed my position for the start of my routine. Facing the audience in an all-black costume with only my eyes not shrouded in black, I knelt with my head down and arms extended in front of me. As theatrical fog moved across the stage, the music began, and the main curtain opened. Slowly, I raised my head to see hundreds of women sitting at tables and looking to be entertained.

Rising and moving smoothly, I began my routine. After a few slow martial arts moves low to the ground, I stood up, paused, and peeled back my head cover to a good response from the audience and early urgings to "take it off." Finger by finger, I slowly took off my gloves, tossing each one aside. I looked at the audience and made eye-to-eye contact with a few women which settled me focus on the audience. I began to feel a connection with them and, as my confidence and feel for the audience developed, I felt more rhythm and flow. I positioned myself centre stage and close to the front to take off my top. With encouragement from the audience and timing it to a sudden change in the music, I ripped open my top to show my chest, slid it slowly off my arms and tossed it aside to a loud response. I then moved onto swinging the double nunchaku, which I was very comfortable with. The grand finale was ripping off my pants in one practised and dramatic movement to another sudden change in the music. There I was, facing 250 women in a strong wide stance, wearing only a leather male G-string, and my dance shoes.

For the last part of the performance, I walked around the tables and climbed up on a couple of them. This was physically risky with wobbly tables, some groping and lots of spilled drinks, but it was dramatic and reduced the time I had to dance on stage. There were women of all ages, shapes, and personalities, including a few who were surprisingly aggressive. Over this part of the performance, some placed five or even ten-dollar bills in my G-string like men do with female strippers and pole dancers. Back on stage at the end of my act I bowed and moved off. I knew I had work to do but was happy with my performance. I was relieved that I had not made a fool of myself, enjoyed it, and knew I would improve.

A dancer from New Zealand I will call T Scott and I formed our own show and moved into a beautiful apartment overlooking Queenscliff beach in Manly. Our apartment was on the first floor with the beach on the other side of the road. I was free of financial stress and living a good life while studying full time. T coached me through my routines, and I found the creative side of it engaging. Where should we fit my routine into our show? What music should I use? What costume should I wear, and I had to decide on the details of timing, positioning and how to relate to the audience.

I took up dance classes with Scott and T at a popular dance school in Broadway. T was a Pakeha (European New Zealander) whose father enrolled him in a rough Māori school to toughen him up. He also boxed at a high level in New Zealand and Australia. Curious about my martial arts background, he wanted to know how to deal with kicks. On a few occasions when we found the time and space at the dance school, we would spar very lightly in a vacant room. Through these sessions he learned to see and deal with kicks above the waist, but I did not do any leg kicks. The odd time someone from the dance school stuck their head in the door, they soon left.

Working as a male stripper for two years got me through my PE degree, but it was a weird world. On a good night, with a big audience there was an energy that I had never experienced before, but the shows where only a handful of women turned up in a big empty space were difficult to endure, and I struggled to pretend I was enjoying it like Scott and T could. By the end of a good show, most of the audience was really pumped up and for about an hour after the show we had elevated status among the women. After that, we were no different to the other men in the room looking to get laid.

Despite living in Central Australia, Greg did not miss out on the stripper experience. He studied dance when he was a teacher in Sydney before he moved to Darwin and the Central Australia. He had a great body that he never stopped working on and was a natural performer. Teaching at Mount Ebenezer (between Alice Springs and Uluru) and then at Pulardi, near Mount Allen, in the Tanami Desert, he had a strong identity as a Territorian. His guest appearances in our show were as the navy officer from the movie, *An Officer and a Gentleman*, and he always blew the audience away.

Greg committed himself to his Aboriginal community at Pulardi and wanted to help bring back the traditional manhood ceremony to give young men a stronger Aboriginal identity. This is why he had two parallel lines cut across his chest by Teddy, who was the Aboriginal elder where Greg worked and lived. Greg felt the scars, as a traditional mark of manhood, were not thick enough, so he asked Teddy to cut them again and put more sand in the wounds to widen the scars. Maybe that is why he smiled so widely when he ripped off his shirt to expose his chest on stage. I wondered how many women in the room knew what those scars were, what they meant and how much pain was involved.

The Turning-point

Sweating in the October sun as I dug out a big rock, I didn't notice Sue until she stopped at the barbed wire fence and said, "You'd better come here, Ric," avoiding eye contact.

Sensing that something was wrong, I dropped the crowbar and walked cautiously to the fence.

"Greg's been killed. The police are here…" she said, turning away.

Shock does not adequately describe how I felt as I followed her up to the family house. Confused and in disbelief, I only managed to ask her, "Are you sure? How? How did he die?"

"On his bike," she replied.

Nauseous, disoriented, and separated from my body, I was aware of every footstep as I walked behind Sue. The birds were quiet, and all I could hear was my mother crying as we approached the house. Her tormented wailing ripped me apart with grief and despair seeping from the house as we walked up the steps, I didn't want to get to that door. The police were leaving through the front door as we entered through the back.

Greg had died on his off-road Yamaha on his way to the Simpson Desert, in an area so remote that his body cooked for two to three days before anyone found him. Finding that out was the worst moment in my life, and there was no escape. Greg lived in Mount Allan, where rumour had it that some Indigenous people driving past saw him lying on the ground near his bike but, thought he was sleeping so drove on. So much about his death was difficult to understand from a brother's and whitefella's perspective.

According to local Mount Allen people, Greg was the victim of *Kurdaitcha*, which are a type of shaman amongst the Arrernte people in Central Australia. Death is willed by them to punish a guilty person, and the area where Greg died is considered to be the heartland of *Kurdaitcha* traditional sorcery. He was either in the wrong place at the wrong time or had unwittingly caused offence and paid the ultimate price.

The four of us spent every day inside the family home, sharing our grief and loss but with no plan or way of dealing with it. Some close friends visited or called to give us support, but nothing they said helped. Once they left or hung up on the phone, the darkness returned. Every morning, I would wake up in the humpy, hoping for a second or two that it was a bad dream but then sink back into my pillow as reality hit me. Unable to think clearly or act effectively, I didn't know what to do, but had to do something.

After a few days of misery, I faced the outside world by venturing into town with a cap and my Ray-ban sunnies on for separation from the outside world. Everybody in town knew of Greg's death and I dreaded seeing people approach me to express their condolences. No matter how determined I was not to blubber and cry, I would lose my composure when anyone said how sorry they were. I began to deal with Greg's death by accepting that he was dead and that physically, he was not coming back.

Mum called Greg Cuddles, and he was her favourite. The powerful, fearless man that he was outside the home would sometimes be like one of her Siamese cats she fussed over so much inside the house. Sitting on the lounge, she would lovingly brush his hair with his head on her lap but outside the family home Greg was a warrior and adventurer. Our battles in the *dojo* and on the rugby-pitch were always intense. Taller than me with a superb physique, he developed an identity as a tough, no-nonsense Territorian over the last six years of his life. The Territory really suited him, but, as much as he loved his life in Central Australia, he had decided to apply for a teaching position that would allow him to move back to the Bay or nearby in 1990. He had wanted to build a house on the McGettigan's Lane property and look after Mum and Dad in their later years. During his 1988 to 1989 Christmas visit, he had cleared lantana and camphor laurel trees where he was going to build it. His friends sometimes visited to help or just drink a mug of his strong billy tea around a fire, and probably share a joint.

Greg and I had set up half a dozen large rocks in a circle, around a smaller circle of rocks for the fire. This circle of sitting rocks around the fireplace was where he conducted his bush tea ritual. After lighting the fire, he shaped it for the billy while everyone found a place to sit down. As we waited for the water to boil, someone would usually roll a joint to be passed around as we talked.

Once the billy came to the boil, Greg tossed in a handful of black bush tea and stirred it with a twig from one of the gum trees. When it was ready, he would pour the brew, taking care to limit the tea leaves going into our chipped, enamel mugs. Everything Greg did was a performance, including the bush tea ritual. We all sat in a circle on our rocks with the lingering smell of the fire as it died down, and the happy sounds of warbling magpies in the surrounding trees. He created the scene and shaped the dialogue in a mix of leadership and warm friendship. He no longer had anything to prove to me, our parents or anyone else. He had discovered who he was and found purpose in life.

Greg graduated from New England University in Armidale as a secondary school geography teacher during a shortage of primary school teachers in NSW. After completing a retraining course, he took his first teaching position in a Liverpool (Sydney) primary school. Living on the coast at Stanwell Tops, he found life was good for him, but he yearned for adventure.

After arriving back in Sydney from a big bike 'tour', he took a teaching job in Darwin. He took his Siamese cat up to Byron Bay for Betty to adopt and headed off to Darwin for a year. He enjoyed the Territory so much that he then took a job teaching in Central Australia. Greg spent three years at Mount Ebenezer, which is between Alice Springs and Uluru. He then took a position as Visiting Outstation Teacher at Pulardi school, near Mt Allen Station, in the Tanami Desert. Respected and loved by the local Aboriginal community, he was a man of immense energy and enthusiasm who immersed himself in his teaching job and his obligation to work for, and with, his community.

After his death, his mob followed the traditional practice of not using his name to avoid recalling and disturbing his spirit. In any reference to him, they used his substitute name of *Kumantjayi*. The ongoing wailing of the women grieving for him was unheard of and especially for a whitefella because it is a traditional ritual of Aboriginal mortuary rites. He had an Aboriginal girlfriend who visited his caravan at Mount Allen regularly. After his death, she joined a community of grieving widows called a sorry camp.

Greg thought he'd found corporate sponsorship to take his school community to see and experience the ocean, but it fell through. His university friend, Damien, funded the trip himself. He took every boy and girl in his Pulardi school to Byron Bay to see the ocean for the first time. The elders all went, and it was filmed for a current affairs type program shown over two weeks. One interview with him early in the first episode was recorded at a water hole in the Tanami Desert. He had his mini-mal (8-foot surfboard) with him. Wearing only his board shorts and plenty of zinc cream on his face he sprinted toward his board that he had placed it in the water, jumped onto it and drove it for a few metres in the water before falling off. His enthusiasm in the interview for something he was passionate about was well captured.

The Pulardi mob flew from Alice to Brisbane, which was the first time in a plane for all of them. They travelled by bus down to Byron Bay via the inland route so they would not see the ocean until they got there. A northerly wind was blowing when they arrived, so they took the Pulardi mob to Tallow for their first sight of the ocean. Old Teddy walked into the surf and scooped up a handful of sea water to taste, but quickly spat it out.

Greg had established himself in Pulardi and made a name for himself in the Bay as a local Bay boy doing some impressive work in the Territory. Early in 1989, when home in the Bay, he asked me to visit him at Mount Allen so he could show me his life in the desert.

"I went down to Sydney to see how you live," he said. "I know your debauched lifestyle well, but you don't know about mine."

"You're right, Chidley (nickname), and I'd love to see where you live, but I'm a bit short of cash at the moment."

"Okay, I'll pay your fare out and you just pay your return fare. How does that sound?"

"Can't say no to that!"

Greg had found meaning and purpose through his teaching, adventure and achievements in the Territory, and I was impressed. He wanted me to know about his life in the desert, to show me what he had done and share his lifestyle with me. He was going to get an extra bike so we could do some serious riding and strengthen our brotherly bond. I was up for it.

He planned for this trip to occur during his holidays and at a time when I could go, but we did not count on the 1989 national pilots' strike. Able to find a flight to Alice but not a return flight, I didn't go. Disappointed, Greg decided to do our trip he had planned on his own. He had always kept detailed diaries, so we were able to trace his journey and the last days of his life.

Greg decided to explore one of the few tracks that he had not ridden on the way to the Simpson Desert. He met some Brits travelling in a car with whom he shared a few joints and conversation. By the time he was set to depart, it was getting dark so they suggested he ride on a better road that they would travel on and take advantage of their car's head lights. Declining the offer, he took off on his own—out into the darkness and emptiness of the desert, as he had done so many times before. The route he planned involved heading northeast of Alice Springs along the unsealed Plenty Highway, crossing into Queensland, heading south and then down into South Australia. He would then cross the Simpson Desert before coming out onto the Stuart Highway and heading North to Alice Springs in one giant loop.

On his many tours Greg and his mates regularly came off their bikes. He told me that nobody was ever hurt and that they would just laugh loudly about it, then get back on their bikes and roar off. He was skilled at spotting bulldust-filled holes on the dirt tracks he travelled on and avoiding them. Bulldust is extremely fine, powder-like dust that settles in holes in the road, making them very difficult to see. He would drive up the berm to bypass the potholes he spotted and then back down onto the road. On his final ride, he did not see the last one.

The police told Bill that Greg's tracks showed how he moved up on the bank of the road to avoid the bulldust filled potholes, then came back down on to the road, but one hole too early. His front wheel dropped into the big hole which flipped him off his bike. Coming off his bike like this was reasonably common for him, but this time it was different. Propelled up in the air, his bike came down on his neck, killing him instantly. Or so the police told Bill. Betty could not bring herself to see his body or talk to the police.

I had a couple of dreams about Greg after his death and occasionally still do, but they are not as real as the early ones. The first one I had was so real that I am not sure it was a dream. We were enjoying one of those conversations where everything feels perfect, and you just could not feel any better, but suddenly I realised that he had died and wondered how I could be talking to him.

"What are you doing here, Greg?" I said. "You're dead."

"Don't worry about it, Ric," he casually replied. "It's cool."

Trying to make sense of what was going on in the dream, I woke up. Was it really a dream? If not, what was it? That was over thirty years ago, but as Indigenous Australian, Miriam-Rose Ungunmerr-Baumann from Daly River, southwest of Darwin, suggests, we own our grief and allow it to heal slowly.

My last clear memory of Greg is of us chatting over coffee during the Christmas break at one of the new cafés that were popping up in the Bay over the late eighties. It was after we'd had a great surf at The Pass with good positive vibes and enjoyable, comfortable conversation.

"Ric, if I die before you, I want you to do something for me."

"Why do you think you're going to die before me? Why are you even talking about death anyway? You're at the peak of your life, Chidley."

"Who knows when your time is up? Do you? Will you do something for me or not?"

"Of course, I will."

"I want my body cremated and my ashes released at the end rock."

"Okay. I can do that. If I ever need to."

The end rock was where we sat on our boards waiting for waves and to earn right of way by being on the inside paddling for waves over the late sixties and early seventies. With Bill so sceptical of religion, we had no death rituals to follow, which made Greg's clarity about what we should do with his body invaluable. The Pass had always been a special place for us, and this gave it spiritual meaning for our entire family. It was also a measure of Greg's love for the Bay and the strength of his identity with it. Making sense of death is a challenge that is beyond me, but I know how much I miss his company. He would have been my wife's brother-in-law, Amy's uncle, a father, and a husband. He would have excelled in all these roles.

The pilots' strike meant that my parents had to drive 3000 kilometres from Byron Bay to Alice Springs to identify Greg's body and then back. They had to travel close to 6000 kilometres in one week in the heat of the desert. I can't imagine what they endured to get there and back. What did they talk about for all those hours in the car?

News of Greg's death spread around town quickly, but Bill had no plans for a church service. He just shut down under the stress of losing his son. His ability to deal with any problem calmly and effectively always impressed me, but Greg's death was too much for him.

After picking up Greg's ashes at the Byron Bay post office I sat opposite it in my car, separated from the world outside. Just me with Greg's ashes in a plastic box on my lap and still hoping that this was just a bad dream. So many rich experiences I had shared with him flooded my mind, and I asked myself, how that life, energy and presence could be reduced to a cold plastic box of ashes? Was this all that remained of this larger-than-life man and brother of mine?

I let people know that we were having a dawn farewell for Greg at The Pass. His friends gathered in silence as the sun rose over the small, smooth waves moving gently along the beach from The Pass. Bill, our friend, Ned, and I carried our boards to the water, and I had the plastic box of Greg's ashes. We waded into gentle and welcoming ocean and then paddled in silence toward the end rock. I felt the heaviness of grief but was healing, and my senses were alive. I felt the energy of nature around me and was sensuously aware as my hands sliced the coolness of the water and pulled through it on each stroke.

Sitting on my board at the end rock, I emptied Greg's ashes into the water and watched them drift downward, swirling and disappearing into the ocean.

"Rest in peace, Chidley," I said.

Sad but beautiful, it encouraged me to think more about the spiritual aspect of life—about how physical death might not, or even could not, be the end.

Greg's death was the biggest challenge I had faced in my life, and I could not imagine getting over it at the time. I felt better after releasing his ashes at The Pass, but grief came back to weigh me down as it did when a brief experience of freedom like riding a great wave provided momentary relief.

I knew that I could not change the past and began to think about how I could shape what is to come. Moving toward 1990, there was not much to celebrate for our family with the 1989 Christmas being the first without Greg. We continued our tradition of the annual long family joint, but it felt forced. His energy was sorely missed.

Slowly, my life seemed to be slowly moving back toward normal as I dealt with the suffering and looked to focus on the present and play what was in front of me. I was rebuilding my karate club, looking forward to the rugby season as the first-grade coach and regularly surfing again.

During his visit to Australia from Japan earlier in 1989, I had a long conversation with my former karate student, David. After talking about karate and Japan, I told him I had completed a level 2 rugby coaching qualification in Brisbane with Queensland Rugby and that I was going to coach the Byron Bay first grade team. David knew little about rugby and less of my involvement in it until this conversation. Not too long after Greg's death, David called me to tell me that his university in Osaka was looking for an Australian or New Zealand rugby coach and, because he was Australian, they asked him if he knew of anyone. After hearing that his karate *sensei* might be a good candidate, they wanted to interview me. If I was offered the job, would I be prepared to move from Byron Bay to Osaka? I had just realised my goal of becoming a PE teacher in my hometown and after losing my brother and felt an obligation to be around for the family.

Betty was pleased that the university wanted to interview me, but I could sense her wanting me to stay home and could very well understand why. Later, I had a conversation with Bill over a cup of tea on the veranda about it and he told me to go.

"How many opportunities to be a professional rugby coach do you think you are going to get in your lifetime, Ric? You can't pass up this opportunity. We'll be right. You go."

My 'gut' told me to go. I was only on a contract at the local high school, and a job like this would offer me something to focus on as a way of negotiating the grief I was experiencing. It might also be time for me to set higher goals, and what an opportunity to develop my karate!

David and Barnsey met me at the old Itami Airport and drove me to my accommodation, but not before we had something to eat and a few beers at a small local restaurant. The master and staff all knew them well and there was a lot of laughing and good cheer with some of the conversation about me and me being interviewed. I did not understand anything they said, but I felt comfortable. It was a taste of Osaka and I loved it. Despite not speaking any Japanese, I felt very comfortable in this warm little restaurant and thought to myself what a blast it would be if I got the job and ended up living here!

David told me our hosts were impressed that the university had flown me in from Australia for an interview and pleased for me that I was being considered for such an important coaching position. He said to them that I knew how important the position was and would do my best.

When I first agreed to fly to Japan for the interview, I wasn't sure I wanted the job. At a level somewhere between the conscious and the non-conscious, I was just going to escape grief and for a free visit to Japan, but, halfway through the conversations at the restaurant, I felt in my *tanden* that I wanted the job. I started to realise the opportunity for a life changing experience that was within reach.

I then shared my concerns with David about not having enough coaching experience at a highly competitive level such as in the Kansai A League that the university competed in. I asked David how I might compare to other applicants and how I should present myself. He said that he did not really know too much about the competition, or about rugby but he knew that they were tired of finishing at the bottom of the ladder. If they appointed someone with a good profile and climbed up the ladder it would also attract more high-quality players from the better rugby high schools.

As we talked, I found out that if I got the job, I would work under the Director of Rugby with half a dozen assistant coaches. For eleven months of the year, I would be responsible for a squad of at least eighty players with expectation that the university's team would work its way up the rankings. The university fielded as many teams as possible for practice games that were played all year, but the A Team contested the end of year *League Sen* games where one loss could be catastrophic.

As the conversation continued, I began to lose a little confidence in my ability to handle such a long and complex year and the responsibility that I would have for results. I had gone from gladly accepting the offer for an interview but not being so sure I wanted the job to deciding I did really want it, and then self-doubt about being able to do it. I decided not to worry too much about what I couldn't do and focus on my strengths. If I didn't get the job, I would still enjoy the visit and have both my Byron Bay coaching position and karate teaching to go back to.

The interview questions did not focus much on my coaching experience. With David acting as interpreter, a lot of the questions were about values, character, discipline, and my work ethic. We talked about karate and what David was like when he started karate with me in Lismore. They also asked about my desire to live in Japan and how I thought I could deal with such a different culture. It seemed to me that they were happy about the prospect of having an Australian rugby coach with a background in karate.

I expected another half an hour of questioning, but the interview finished early. There were long moments of silence, nodding, sucking of teeth and brief discussions that I did not understand. My feel for the interaction and was that there was agreement on something. Was it that I was not at all suitable or very suitable? All eyes turned to David with the person who seemed to be leading the process saying something to him.

David then turned to me: "They want to know if you can start tomorrow."

"Are they offering me the job?"

"Yes."

The package included a good salary and a great apartment in East Osaka. I told David that I was very happy to accept the offer of the job and was looking forward to it but had to go home to tidy up my affairs. I told him I could be back in a month. At the completion of the meeting, they gave me a big wad of cash to enjoy a few days in Osaka and take a good memory home with me.

How odd life can be, I thought, in the plane on the way home. I had gone from the satisfaction and feeling of achievement returning to the Bay for a casual PE teaching position with a degree to the abject despair of losing my brother, and now this.

Challenge and Change in Japan

Eighty players formed a big circle with all eyes on me as their new, and foreign, coach. I knew how many players I would have well before our first session but was still surprised when I faced them. Eighty players stood in one big circle on dry, hard packed dirt and not a blade of grass in sight.

"Okay, as one group, jog around the ground four times, and then we will do some stretching," I said loudly while making a large circle in the air with my right index finger.

They looked at each other, at their captain, and then at me. I walked about 10 metres out toward the centre of the circle and ran around in a small circle, stopped, and held up four fingers and yelled "RUN FOUR TIMES!"

The captain understood immediately and called out in a deep, powerful voice "YONSHU HASHITE!" Eighty players then repeated in unison with amazing power—"YONSHU HASHIMASU!" and started jogging.

Well, here we go, I said to myself, as they all moved off in a very orderly manner.

We trained every day of the week. Before this, I met with the captain and a group of fourth year players in my office to plan the session. I used what Japanese I had learned, and what little English they knew but relied most on the illustrations in my Queensland rugby training manual. Communication was not really a significant problem, but the style of rugby they had learned to play was. I could see that I had a few challenges to meet but was confident I could do it and felt enthusiasm for the task. I saw a big opportunity to transform how the university played rugby.

The better players were on sport scholarships at university, while the rest were normal fee-paying students who wanted to join a club. As coach at Byron Bay, I was elated if fifteen players turned up, but, in Osaka, I had 80 on a packed dirt field, 2/3 the size of a normal rugby pitch. The large number of players suited traditional

Japanese training with endless repetition that tested and developed their tolerance, tenacity, and courage.

The first-year students in my club had to be at training more than an hour before their seniors to prepare for the session. This included pumping up 20 to 30 rugby balls that they had deflated after training the day before. By my second year as coach, my Japanese had improved enough to communicate with the players, so I asked the first years who were pumping up the balls why they had to do it.

"It helps them stay in good condition longer," one of them explained.

"Really?"

"Yes, it is good for the balls."

If one of the seniors' headbands or head scarves fell off during training, the nearest junior player would rush over to pick it up and pass it to him with a quick but deep bow and apology before rushing off to re-join play. In a four-year university program, fourth years were like kings and first years like grovelling peasants who had to suffer and work their way up the ladder to earn their place. They had the same experience over three years of junior high school and then three years of senior high school—start at the bottom and work your way up to the top then start at the bottom again at the next level up. Before I arrived, the A team was chosen only from fourth years because they had earned it through what they had to put up with from first year to fourth year.

Bill and Betty flew to Japan from Byron Bay for two weeks and saw two of the *League Sen* (Championship) matches. When I saw them emerge with their luggage at the airport, the changes in my life made it feel like I had not seen them for so long, yet it had been less than a year. My father's handshake and my mother's long hug reminded me of how important my family was to me. They were full of questions, and, as I answered them, I felt proud of where I was and what I was doing. After Betty's concern with me accepting the job in Osaka so soon after Greg's death, she had a very positive attitude toward my life in Japan. She seemed amazed at the environment I was living in, my command of Japanese and my success as a coach. They were amazed with everything, and there was little talk of Greg apart from them suggesting how he would have followed me to Japan and how taken he would have loved Japanese women.

"Wouldn't Greg have loved this?" Betty said wistfully.

"Oh yes," said Bill. "Right up his Alley. The rugby, karate, the adventure. And the very cute Japanese girls."

At the first *League Sen* match with my parents in the stand, I had a moment when I was reminded of what I had achieved and how I had made the right decision in coming to Osaka. There I was, sitting up in the coaches' area at a packed stadium in my navy-blue blazer, University tie and grey slacks.

In preparation for their visit to Osaka, Bill had practised diligently with chopsticks by picking up peas and was able to eat most of his meals with them. Betty did not even try, so she had to carry a knife, fork, and spoon in her handbag when we went out for a meal. I could not remember seeing my father so energetic and stimulated as he was for the two weeks that he and Betty spent with me. He didn't even complain about sleeping on a futon on the tatami floor or having to get it out of the cupboard every night and put it back the next morning. As it was for me on my first visit to Japan, every day for Bill and Betty was exciting, baffling, and stimulating. I felt happy for them, and for myself.

My parents also met my girlfriend, Chiho, who I had told them about over the phone and in letters I had written and sent to them. Both were excited to meet her and liked her very much, particularly my father.

I worked with the fourth years over my first year to making gradual changes because I couldn't speak Japanese. We had a very successful year, and everyone was looking forward to the next season. A couple of the assistant coaches I had dinner with one night said that they wish I had been the coach when they played for the university. Flushed with my success, a better command of Japanese and growing confidence in my second year, I decided to adopt a more Australian approach to coaching and how we played. Central to this plan was a tour of Australia which would be the first overseas tour by any university club. Getting it to happen with my limited Japanese was demanding and a significant achievement for me.

The tour group comprised about 60 players, a large group of old boys, the director and his family. We played games in Brisbane against Queensland University 4th grade and Bond University on the Gold Coast, but the highlight of our tour was when we fielded three teams to play against teams from Mullumbimby and Byron Bay. The Japanese boys were smaller but quicker, and much fitter. They were brave, with good skills, but had little vision, made poor decisions and lacked creativity. Still, with much beer consumed after the games were completed, there was a lot of good energy and positive interaction.

Departing, I was on the lead bus as it moved slowly past people waving goodbye which included most of the Byron Bay team. They seemed too organised to me, and I wondered what they were doing. That was until they all turned away from the bus as we passed, dropped their pants and underwear to expose their buttocks, bent over, and spread their cheeks to expose their anuses.

The Byron Bay team had given us a team brown eye performed with more precision than any of their set plays on the field, and the Japanese boys were stunned. They thought it was a deep insult.

"What is the meaning?"

"What did we do wrong?"

"Why are they doing that?" different players asked me as I felt caught between two cultures.

I tried to explain this odd cultural practice in Japanese and told them that it means they like you. "They are not being rude. It's a joke. It's very difficult to explain. The two cultures are so different."

Our tour finished in Sydney where we watched the Wallabies defeat the All Blacks and headed back to Japan the next day. I had hoped to build on this exposure to rugby outside Japan and take the team up a notch in performance, but we did no better than the previous year.

My third year of coaching was my worst, despite a bit of help from a couple of very experienced international players. Matt was a Queensland Reds prop helping me coach the forwards and legendary All Black, Buck Shelford was famous in Japan. I interpreted for him on a short coaching tour in Japan, and he returned the favour by doing a scrum session with my players. There was an issue with how the front row of the scrum engaged. I wanted them to change but was unable to convince them and hoped they would listen to Buck Shelford. He had a God-like status in Japan and the players were all very excited to meet him but still would not change. I probably should have backed off but was determined to have them change the way the front row of the scrum bound, which did not help my relationship with the players.

My final year as coach was disappointing enough for me and the university to part company. Chiho and I then moved in together, and I worked at an English Language school for a year, which was quite a step down for me, but the following year, through a karate connection, I landed a position as a teacher in an elite level private school, and we moved south to Matsunohama. The name means Pine Beach in English, but there were no pines, no beach visible, and no access to the water. Whatever beaches and trees that used to be in Osaka Bay were long gone and the bay was disgustingly polluted.

Not long after my appointment, I was approached by two students from the rugby team who asked me to coach them. I didn't want to, but I felt their desperation and hope. The boys in the club had never played rugby before and were only allowed to play for two years because, as senior high students (last three years) in one of the best academic school in Osaka, they had to quit rugby in their final year to prepare for exams.

They were small, but very intelligent, curious, and open to learning. We won our first game, and the following Monday I was surprised at how many teachers congratulated me. That was until I said to a colleague, "So, it seems that the rugby team doesn't often win," to which he replied, "They never win. I've been here a long time and don't remember them ever winning a game, and that's why everybody is so happy."

The annual Osaka Fu rugby tournament was for the greater Osaka region, which has a population of eight million and hundreds of schools competing. Getting ready for the first game was like a scene from an American movie with The Nerds (us) playing against the Lummoxes. My boys were short, skinny, and intelligent with none of the arrogance or 'swagger' of their opponents. The opposition players were not only big, but also overweight, and full of arrogance.

The opposing team sneered at us and seemed to make a few disparaging jokes but were not laughing at half time with the Nerds leading. They were certainly not laughing at full time when we beat them by a good margin. Heads down, they walked off, dragging and knowing they would get a good spray from their coach. My boys were politely elated and looking forward to the next game. Every game they played was similar, with brains winning over brawn until we made it to the top thirty teams in Osaka Fu. This was as far as we progressed, but there was great joy at defying the low expectations of everyone. It was my most enjoyable season of rugby coaching ever, and, during the following year, I took the team to Australia on a tour that included a match against Byron Bay High School. I also organised another Osaka high school team's Australian tour of southeast Queensland and Byron Bay the next year but had nothing to do with coaching them.

Over my six years in Japan, I trained regularly in karate, was graded twice and competed in a few tournaments but when I first walked in the Linden *dojo* in Osaka, it had been a few years since I had done any serious, sustained karate training. I did however have a reputation that preceded me because of David who had become a big, powerful opponent and the only non-Japanese to win the All-Japan karate championships. Everybody respected him and many feared him, with the assumption being that his aggression and dynamic skill originated in his training with me back in Australia.

I did most of my training at Linden *dojo* in the lively area of Dotonbori with Hamaguchi Sensei who we *gaijin* (foreigners) referred to among ourselves as 'The Guch'. Friday night training was always spirited enough to earn a hot bath in the nearby public bathhouse and a few beers at the end of the week. When it came to sparring on my first Friday night, it seemed like everybody was gunning for me. My speed, fitness, and timing were off, and I felt under siege. Opponent after opponent came at me hard with some heavy clashes, strong hits to my body and one well delivered and controlled kick to my face that gave me a bloody nose. At the end of the session, my nose was bleeding a little and I was exhausted but enjoyed the hard session as a welcome to karate training in Japan.

The next week, we used bullet proof face guards that allowed contact to the face and seemed like a signal from the Guch to go for it. Sparring was very lively, and I had some good exchanges. Toward the end of the sparring, my face guard was fogging up so badly that I didn't recognise my opponent. He was wearing a white belt but was more aggressive than I expected. I hit him with a left foot roundhouse kick to his midsection and felt it do a little damage. As he stepped back, I followed with a stronger right footed roundhouse kick to his ribs that dropped him. He lay moaning on the floor, and when I lifted my face guard, I saw that it was one of the American blackbelts in the club who had left his belt at home.

"Oh, sorry, Paul. I didn't know it was you, with my mask fogged up."

"That's okay, Ric. I'll be fine after I get my breath back. Pretty strong kick that last one. Nice one."

After about 30 seconds he got up, exhaled, and rested with his hands on his knees before standing upright. I felt satisfied with the technique and timing of my kicks but was glad he was not injured. Sparring could get aggressive at times, but punches and kicks were usually not thrown in anger. This aspect of training helped develop me develop strong friendships and mutual respect between myself and my fellow students in the Linden *dojo*.

In what became a ritual for me over six years, we all walked down the alleyway behind the Linden dojo, in a red-light district to the bath house. On our way we walked past a range of odd little businesses that catered for diverse sexual interests and perversions. On Friday nights, we would go to the same local bath house that allowed men with tattoos in, which was unusual because most men with tattoos were *yakuza* or connected with them. When in the same bath, we did not talk to them, and they did not talk to us, but I was always aware of them. There was always a feeling of careful awareness and respect both ways but no verbal interaction.

After the class, we went to a local *izakaya* and started with a toast and drinking a mouthful of cold beer from a big *dainama* (a litre glass of draft beer). Sitting down at the counter or a table, we would order food and beer as we needed it. I enjoyed the food, beer, the lively conversations, the comfortable company, and loved the energy of the places we ate in.

The trains stopped at midnight, but, for the first three years, I rode my mountain bike to training from East Osaka. One Friday night, while I was racing home on my bike at about 1.00 am with my *gi* in a backpack, the police pulled me over. As I stopped, I was nervous. Would I be in some sort of trouble for riding a pushbike over the limit?

"Do you speak Japanese?" the policeman asked.

"Yes, but not so well."

"It's good enough, it seems."

"I do my best."

"Do you have any ID?"

"Yes, in my bag."

'What else is in your bag?"

"My karate *dogi* and belt," I said, pulling out my *dogi* rolled up and tied with my belt.

This immediately caught their attention with a couple of nodding heads, and I felt the mood lighten. They asked what school of karate I trained with, a few more questions about how long I had been training, how long I had been in Japan and what work I did. Gradually, I felt relaxed, and conversation flowed more freely. They were impressed with my rugby coaching position and, after quickly looking at my passport, asked me a few questions about how my team was doing and about rugby in Australia. They then told me to do my best and take care getting home. The pleasant exchange put me in a good mood, and I peddled off toward home at pace.

For my second three years in Osaka, I had moved and had to make sure I got on the last train. I saw many men who were excessively drunk and struggling to stay upright vomit in the train or on the platform. One Friday night, I stood watching a very drunk salaryman (white collar worker employed in a company) who was asleep on one of the long bench seats with his head against the window and leaning toward a woman who was sitting bolt upright next to him. He was semi-conscious at best, with his head vibrating against the window and leaning toward the uncomfortable looking woman next to him. I could feel her discomfort and her anxiety with subtle glances his way. If I had been in her place, I would have moved because he looked likely to throw up before long, and, ten minutes out of Namba, he suddenly vomited on the window, with some of it spilling onto the woman. Horrified, she jumped to her feet and moved away from him in one swift movement but said nothing as she found something in her bag to wipe the few droplets of vomit from her sleeve and shoulder. Nobody in the carriage said anything, and the drunk was oblivious to what he had done. There was only very subtle and brief eye-to-eye communication between passengers and people giving him more space. It reminded me of how restrained Japanese people usually are in public.

Once I regained fitness and reconnected with karate, I enjoyed training and was very happy to be back into it. I trained three or four nights a week and started to really understand it, in its natural context. Over six years in *Hayashi-Ha* karate, I was graded from third dan to fourth dan and then to fifth dan by Soke, who was one of the great modern Japanese masters. He had amazing presence and was intimidating when I trained with him in the *hombu* (headquarters). I barely spoke to him but had huge respect for him and was elated to be graded by him.

My introduction to learning from Hashimoto Sensei was like something from the movie *The Karate Kid*. I went to his *dojo* to ask if he would teach me *kata*.

"What's your favourite *kata*?" he asked me.

I named the most difficult and complex one I could do.

"Oh, is that so?" he said. "Show me."

When I finished, he laughed and made fun of my movements by exaggerating them. He drew my attention to some very basic yet important movements I didn't know much about.

I didn't know what to say so just kept saying "yes, I understand, I'm sorry."

"Which *kata* can you do well?" he then asked me, and I told him the most basic one as a joke, but he asked me to show him. I was a fourth dan black belt at the time and this was the first kata an absolute beginner had to learn. I was confident I would do it well and wanted to make up for the first one I had done so poorly.

When I finished, he looked at me and waited for three to four seconds before speaking.

"That's better," he said with a subtle nod, "but still not good enough."

"Yes, I understand," I replied. "I'm sorry,"

He explained some basic movement that generated power from the feet and through the hips that should be evident in the *kata*. After a couple of attempts, I understood what he meant.

"How does that feel?" he asked me each time I performed the move. "Can you feel the difference?"

I was starting to realise how limited my knowledge of *kata* was and how important it is. He then told me to find some space in the *dojo* and practise on my own. I was a little embarrassed but not offended or discouraged. Instead, I had a hunger to learn and was beginning to realise how important humility is for learning.

The mood in Hashimoto Sensei's classes was relaxed, with his students calm, focused and seeming to enjoy every class. I had a lot to learn but over the first few weeks felt like I was not improving. Week by week, Hashimoto spent more time with me as I showed humility, put in the effort needed, listened attentively and became more aware of my body and its movement. This was learning that changed my approach to karate, helped me be more reflective and promoted more inner learning for me. It was also a good life lesson.

Tall, flexible, and athletic, Hamaguchi Sensei was loose, relaxed, and open minded. He taught *kata* but was much better at *kumite*, having made the final of the world karate championships one year. He got on well with all the *gaijin* students and took an interest in our lives outside karate. I came to respect him as a *sensei* and to like him very much as a man.

He spoke on my behalf at our engagement party in Osaka and later gave me some good advice: "Don't waste your time in Japan picking up Japanese girls and drinking beer, Richard. Take the opportunity to improve yourself while you are here and take something home to advance yourself back in your country and make you a better person."

The Japanese notion of a mysterious red thread that connects life-long partners in Japan provides an explanation for me of how I met Chiho. Breaking my nose during my karate grading in Hong Kong, almost a decade before I moved to Japan, I had an opportunity to have it straightened in the biggest private hospital in Osaka that was owned by the university where I coached.

Chiho was PA for the hospital's chief administrator and the first person I met with in his department. She was stunning, and I was doing my best to make conversation as she walked me down the hospital corridors. The next time I saw her was at a little kiosk in the hospital after my operation with me wearing a *yukata* (Japanese style hospital robe) and wearing a face mask with a visibly swollen and discoloured face, I asked if she remembered me. Smiling demurely, she quietly said she did and then excused herself with a hint of a giggle. Back at work as coach, I asked a junior player who lived near the hospital to take her flowers for me and on Hamaguchi *Sensei's* advice invited her to a rugby practice game.

From then on, we gradually got to know each other and started going out. I had previously only had one steady girlfriend and the slow pace of getting to know her felt like the start of a long relationship. Over the first two years of our relationship, we lived together but kept our relationship a secret from her mother. Her mum had hoped Chiho would marry a doctor, but the closest she had been to a *gaijin* was when a few foreigners ran through her mountain village in a marathon. Our relationship developed enough over three years for us to want to get married, so I sought advice from the Guch about how to approach Chiho's mother.

"First, travel to where her mother lives and knock on her door, but she probably won't answer so you will have to go home. Then go back and try again and if she still won't talk to you try a third time. If it's no good, talk to me again."

Chiho's mum Yayoi lived in a small village of 800 people on a mountain, near a famous Buddhist settlement (Koyasan) established in 805. It was extremely difficult for me to get there from Osaka, but Chiho had an alternative plan. She invited her mum to stay at our place before going to the hospital the next day for a check-up. Chiho went out to meet her mother at the train station while I prepared dinner that I would serve with a bottle of Australian wine. It would certainly be easier than the possible three mammoth trips to her mum's place in the mountains that the Guch suggested.

Chiho's mum was questioning her about who was inside her apartment as she removed her shoes in the *genkan* (entrance).

"There's somebody in there," she said a bit alarmed. "I can hear them!"

"It's okay," Chiho said. "Just take off your shoes and go inside."

"Why is someone inside? Who is it...?"

Giggling a little, Chiho gently pushed her mum into the room from the *genkan* for her to find herself facing me in an apron, with spatula in hand. There was an awkward pause that I broke by bowing and greeting her in Japanese.

Halfway through dinner, Yayoi approved of me, adding, "Of course, I can't oppose (your relationship)."

I thanked her.

Our engagement party was in Osaka early in 1995, and we were married in Byron Bay. It was good to be back home in the Bay for our wedding, surrounded by friends, relatives, and Chiho's family for probably the most important event in my life. In my speech at the reception, I used a rugby analogy to say that I had played poorly in the first half of my life, but that I was going to lift my game in the second half.

"As long as you kick a few goals!" Bill shouted, bringing the house down.

Bill saw our marriage as an aspect of healing after the Pacific War and looking to the future instead of dwelling on the dreadful past. He had lost most of his army mates in the Philippines and might have perished there as well had he not been pulled out of his regiment to work in Intelligence.

On one of his trips to Osaka, we talked over dinner with one of my assistant coaches whose father had been a boy in Osaka when it was bombed by the allies. Bill was very happy to gain a first-hand human perspective from the other side. When talking about Chiho and me getting married, he told me he had a dream of us moving back into the humpy. "I can see your brown skinned children playing in the creek," he told me.

Chiho's mother had expressed concern with the security of my work as a rugby coach and encouraged me to think about our future, which is something I had never really done. I left my professional rugby coaching job but stayed in Osaka after meeting Chiho and enrolled in an off-campus master's degree in physical education. My study was on how high school rugby in Japan prepares young men for Japanese work culture and the larger society. It involved reading a great deal on Japanese history, culture, education, and society, and the more I learned about my environment, the more I wanted to learn.

My master's degree took me three years part time to complete. I spent many hours every day, sitting at my little desk with our cat, Tiger, sitting beside my boxy, classic Apple computer and enjoying the 'vibe' of my concentration. This continued after the horrific Great Hanshin Earthquake in 1995 that occurred across Osaka Bay and destroyed the city of Kobe, killing 6000 people. I will never forget that thirty seconds of violent shaking from exactly 6.00 am on January 17 and seeing the destruction wreaked by the earthquake on the TV.

Over the months of aftershocks, Tiger always let me know

when one was coming. Sitting on my desk when I was working, he would pick up approaching aftershocks well ahead of me.

"Here it comes," he told me with his eyes wide open, after which I would feel it coming up from the depths of the earth, wondering if this was going to be another big one.

When it settled down and the building stopped shaking, I got back to work, and Tiger went back to what looked like a meditative state.

For the first time in my life, I enjoyed study, and when I submitted my master's thesis, I felt lost. Three years of discovery and learning had woken me up intellectually, and now I missed it. Thinking about what I could do next, I contacted my supervisor who had just taken a professor's position at the University of Queensland. He told me that if I wanted to do a PhD with him, he would set it up. A PhD? Me, the boy who was expelled from school in Year 12 and failed his first semester at teachers' college? For the first time, I was thinking seriously about the future and where I wanted us to be in ten years' time. I talked with Chiho about it, and she was up for the adventure.

A Career for the New Millennium

I started reading a book written by French sociologist, Pierre Bourdieu but, by the end of the first page hadn't understood what I had read. I read it again but without much more understanding and, after a third reading, I was worried about being smart enough to do what I had come home to do. I took the book to my favourite café where I had a coffee, and another crack at it.

I had made a big decision to give up an enjoyable life in Osaka and bring Chiho to Australia to complete my PhD, but was I capable? Going back to Japan was not an option now, so I kept at it and soon settled in. Within months, I began to enjoy my growing knowledge and understanding of the problems I had faced as a rugby coach in Japan and the intellectual stimulation from interaction with other PhD students and staff. As my knowledge grew, I enjoyed conversation at Wordsmiths' Café with other PhDs so much that sometimes I thought I should pinch myself.

Every second weekend, Chiho and I drove down to Byron Bay from Brisbane, stayed at the family home, caught up with my friends, and did some surfing. Whenever I visited home after Greg's death, I climbed up to the lookout at The Pass to pay my respects to him and connect with his spirit. No matter where we went, Greg and I had always stayed in touch with our family whether away temporarily or long term. Even when in Japan, I stayed in contact with my parents, and they visited me twice. Growing up, Greg, Sue and I appreciated our parents as we were increasingly exposed to the broken and sometimes dysfunctional families of our friends. I realised how important it had been for me to know that my parents always loved me and were always there to support me, emotionally, and financially. Bill and Betty's pride in me doing a PhD meant a lot to me, and I loved my intellectual discussions on education with my father during our visits to McGettigan's Lane. After his constant disappointment with my academic failures and struggles, overhearing him talk to someone about me with great pride had a very big impact on me.

In June 1997, I watched our daughter Amy come into to this world in Brisbane with Chiho's best friend, Yuko. I felt for Chiho and the pain she endured, but I felt high for the following two to three weeks. Chiho's mum came from Japan to help her over the first six weeks after Amy's birth and having a child helped Chiho adjust to Brisbane. She became a member of a community of mothers with children the same age. When I reflected on my challenges in Japan, I could sympathise with those she faced adapting to Australia.

After three years of committed study, I had completed my PhD and was about to submit my dissertation. I took it to the Head of School to sign off and was confident that I had completed a great thesis in only three years. Sociologist Pierre Bourdieu's work had become central to my study, and I was looking forward to a career as an academic.

"It's all done, Richard. said the Head of School after signing off on my thesis. "Walk up that slope and feel the sun on your back."

My appointment at the University of Melbourne in 2000 provided a good start to my academic career. I was proud to work at such a prestigious institution but disappointed at the state of the physical education program and the lack of research activity on it. Though the university was ranked in the top forty in the world, I found myself in a little pocket of it that had different priorities with very little research conducted and published in our area.

I arrived with a few publications in good journals under my belt from my PhD and was keen to do more. I thought I should try to promote research with step one being to put up the front page of each of my publications on a notice board opposite the lift (elevator) as I had seen done at UQ. I wanted to show what research we were doing to people outside our little area and encourage others in it to publish.

When the elevator doors opened for me the next morning, lists of student names had been pinned over my publications by a colleague who had come into the university directly from high school teaching. She taught in health and took a very practical approach, like having the students in her health classes practise putting condoms on a wooden penis.

I took the student list to Vera's (pseudonym) office and spoke to her: "Vera, did you pin this over the publications I had up there?"

"Yes, she said, looking me in the eye. "That board is for student information."

"There are two boards. Do you use them both for student lists and notices? Where do you put publications and anything else related to research?"

"Look, Richard, what matters here is teaching and preparing students to be good teachers. If you need to show people what you publish you can use the other board."

"I am fine with that. In any department, research and publishing is important, and I am hoping that we will have publications from others here. I also want the students and other staff to know that we do research in our area that informs how and what we teach."

"I don't have time to do anything outside teaching but good luck with it."

During my second year at the university, I was promoted, was developing quickly into a good academic and had aspirations.

One day, I called home to speak to Mum, and Bill answered to tell me that she was in hospital.

"Why?" I asked.

"No need to worry, Ric. She was feeling a little off colour and just needed a rest."

"Are you sure?"

"Yes, of course I am. She'll be back home tomorrow."

I called Mum anyway to ask how she was.

"Nothing serious, Ric, I just felt tired, so I came here for a break. I'm being spoiled here. The staff are very nice. How are you anyway? Are you enjoying Melbourne?"

"Yes, Chiho loves living here and working at Melbourne Uni is great. Amy is growing up very quickly. You won't recognise her next time you see her."

I then talked about some minor issues at work and finished with "Take it easy, Mum. I'll talk to you tomorrow. Love you."

The next morning, I answered my office phone to hear my father's voice. "Your mother died last night."

"What happened?"

Bill struggled to speak and could not answer. He finally hung up.

As I sat there, Bill's few words lingered in my ears. It was January 10—the day before Chiho's birthday—and I was struggling to make sense of what I had just heard. Unable to hold back the tears, I slumped over my desk, confused, shocked, not knowing what to do and so alone. It couldn't have happened to my beautiful and loving mother who had always been there whenever I needed her. I wanted to speak to her. I wanted to share a cup of tea and some of her bikkies on the veranda at home with her.

I called Chiho and told her the news. She was very saddened but in control. I felt grateful to have a family to go home to. When I stopped focusing on my grief, I thought about my father and how difficult it must be for him in that big, empty house on his own. In a house that had once been full of life and buzzing with the energy of three vibrant children and so many pets. And poor Sue, who had relied on Betty so much after Greg's death.

Bill had been the dominant influence on me growing up, but Betty was always there in the background. Always quiet, caring and never judging anyone. My father could be a little selfish and intimidating when he lost his temper, but I can't remember Betty ever being angry. She tried a few times with something like "Oh, you are a naughty boy, Ric... very naughty," but always failed.

I remembered the only time Bill hit me. It was after I called Greg a cunt at the dinner table during a disagreement. Bill belted me with his open hand. My face burned hot and throbbed from the blow.

"Do you know what that word means?" he said firmly as the rest of the family sat in silence.

"No, I heard one of my friends say it."

"Well, go and ask him what it means!"

Greg had been Betty's favourite, and she never recovered from his death. "It's just not right for your child to die before you do," she said to me.

Mum was accepting and very liberal. My father was sensitive but with a tough exterior for protection. Betty knew we all did a few drugs and were sexually active but did not lecture any of us. One Friday night, Bill, Betty, Sue, and I came home from dinner at the Returned Services League club and walked onto the veranda towards Greg's bedroom window, with its subdued lighting.

"Oh, Greg's in his room," Betty had said with a smile, but a few steps later we all froze. The thin, off-white curtains were drawn but the red light silhouetted his sexual encounter for all of us to see. He and his partner were, doing it doggie style, as we all watched, speechless for two to three seconds.

"He's a very naughty boy," Betty said with a hint of pride and a little huff as we withdrew from the performance.

As I found out later, our local doctor had not wanted to tell Bill about Betty's death over the phone, so he drove out to McGettigan's Lane to tell him face to face. Bill was working on one of the cars with the bonnet up, when the doctor arrived and gave him the news. Bill stopped, looked down for a minute and exhaled. The doctor said nothing more as they both dealt with the silence. With moistening eyes, Bill looked up and quietly asked Rob to join him on the veranda for a beer, where he so often sat and chatted with Betty.

Looking at their old photos and listening to stories about how they had fallen in love made me think that Betty and Bill were spiritually connected. They looked like the perfect couple, and she never hid her love for him. In 1966, I took a photo of Bill, Betty, Greg, and Sue on the veranda of our house in Lighthouse Road that captured how satisfied and happy my parents were with their life. Living in a wonderful beachside location, Bill was English Master at the local high school and a highly respected figure in the Bay. They also had three children they loved and were very proud of. In 1966, Bill could not have wished for anything more than what he had, and was living his dream, but in 2001 it had fallen apart.

After Betty's death, Bill could not function but would not let anyone organise anything to do with her funeral. I was so stunned by her death that I did not think about how my father and sister were handling the loss. Grief can be so selfish and lonely. Like when I was first told by Sue that Greg had died, I felt nauseous, disoriented, powerless and without purpose or direction. The little dramas at work I had spoken to her about the night before didn't matter anymore.

Greg and Mum's death reminded me of what is important in

life, and how we can place too much importance on things that don't really matter and are often superficial. There can't be much that is more important than love, family, and home. It reminded me about my place in the big picture. No matter how healthy, successful, or powerful anyone is, death awaits them. Where there is life there will also be death. I learned something about this through the pets I have loved and lost, and I think this is an important reason for children to have pets. I've seen them develop from cute kittens or puppies to adults and then decline until it is time to make that difficult decision to end their life, or to find they have been killed by speeding cars. I can't be sure that these experiences helped me deal with the grief following the death of my brother and mother but suspect they did.

Mum and her brother Peter were very close because of the hardship they faced as children. She had protected him from their alcoholic mother by hiding him in places like the laundry basket and taking the beatings herself. Life had been very trying for them as children and they built a very strong relationship that remained strong over the entirety of their lives. Peter was deeply upset at how we said goodbye to Mum. I was very disappointed and knew how he felt but was torn between an obligation to my mother and consideration of my father.

Mum's death was hard enough to deal with for me without the extra stress of arguing with my father about how she would be farewelled. I felt the anguish of my uncle and asked Bill to reconsider. But he shut down and was unapproachable. For the first time in my life, I felt responsibility for our whole family but was not sure of what to do. I felt it was up to me to give her the farewell that she and all who loved her deserved, but not by arguing with my father who had been her lifelong love. It was one of the most trying times in my life.

We finally said goodbye to Mum at the crematorium with no more than ten people there. It felt so lonely and cold as we watched her coffin pass by on its way to the furnace. I kissed it when it stopped and made a blubbering attempt to say something that could express my gratitude and confirm what a wonderful person she was but, could not find the words. It was a draining experience for me, and I realised that from that point onward, I had responsibility for looking after Bill and Sue, as well as Chiho and Amy.

I organised a farewell for Mum at The Pass. This is what she wanted so she could be with Greg. People heard by word of mouth about the farewell and gathered quietly at dawn as Bill, Sue, and I, paddled out to place her ashes near the end rock, with the light surf and the smooth water. She was now with Greg.

That night, Sue, Chiho and I organised a small wake at the family home in the Lane, which was very helpful for me as a low-key semi-formal farewell. Chiho found photos of Betty over different stages of her life that we put on display to celebrate it. Dealing with the grief from Greg's death had been the biggest challenge in my life to that point, and now it was over my mother. The pensive mood of the gathering, some conversations, a few drinks and feeling we had now given Mum a decent farewell helped me get to sleep that night.

I liked my work as an academic and, after Mum's death, immersed myself in it. Six months after her death, I attended the first International Teaching Games for Understanding (TGfU) Conference in Plymouth, New Hampshire (USA). Meeting and talking with people whose work I had read was a buzz.

During the 'town meeting' at the end of the conference the convenor asked if anyone was interested in organising a second conference, but no one volunteered. I was only a lecturer, so I didn't put my hand up but, upon returning to Melbourne, I made inquiries and decided to give it a go.

Convening an international conference was a big challenge for someone who had only attended half a dozen conferences, but I felt I could do it. Melbourne University had an excellent conference team who made it remarkably easy to organise the conference that attracted 250 people and was a big success for me. After the success of the conference and my growing publication output, my standing in the school grew, and I was promoted.

One day, Rod, whose office was across the hall from mine, dropped an advertisement for a job at associate professor level (one step above my position at the time) on my desk.

"There you go, Cobber," he said.

"Do you think I am up to that level, Rod?" I asked and his reply was,

"For sure, Richard. You'd be very competitive."

Not long after sending my application, I saw an advertisement for a position at the University of Sydney that looked interesting. This position was only at senior lecturer level, but I applied anyway. The other university shortlisted me for the associate professor position, but the interview was indefinitely postponed. After the interview at the University of Sydney, I was offered the job and accepted it. We were off to Sydney.

So Amy could taste beach culture, I enrolled her in the North Steyne Surf Life Saving Club's nippers program. Sunday mornings over the season, there would be up to five hundred nippers at the North Steyne club, training, competing, having fun, and learning about the surf. The nippers program was built around competition, but it was low-key, with an emphasis on fun and learning about the ocean. The younger nippers were restricted to beach events like the sprint that Amy won a bronze medal in at the NSW state championships in her first year. With others her age, Amy gradually worked through the wading race to surf swim events, board and ski paddling, and rescue events as she became more competent in the water.

One summer Sunday after nippers' training, Amy and I went out for a body surf. With waves up to about five or six foot breaking hard on the sand bank, we made our way out the back, swimming against a thumping surf. Duck diving under a heavily breaking wave, I looked across to see Amy teasing the churning water above her as she skimmed over the sand bank and with a few strong dolphin kicks, headed toward the surface behind the breaking wave in one, long and graceful arc. It was a momentary vision of beauty, flow, freedom, and harmony with nature for me. It also confirmed how much I loved being a father, and how much I loved my daughter.

The university had great sport facilities and an active program for attracting elite level sports people, and the Vice Chancellor loved sport. I thought it was a long shot, but I asked him to present at a forum I was organising on youth sport. His reply was immediate and positive, and it was the first time most staff had seen him in our faculty.

With the importance of sport at the university, I saw an opportunity for me to flourish in my new environment. After a year there, I approached the new dean with an idea for boosting international enrolments (mainly study abroad students from the USA) in the faculty with sport playing a big part in it. He liked my proposal. In collaboration with some colleagues, I designed a cluster of four courses on sport, Indigenous sport, drama, and theatre. They were all based on learning though experience in the form of field trips around Sydney with assessment based on their reflection on these experiences. In the first year of the program, international student numbers jumped from eight to two hundred in the faculty and the possibilities seemed endless. I was soon a favourite of the dean but not of the deans of the other faculties that traditionally attracted the bulk of study abroad enrolments and the associated income.

Everything I tried at Sydney University was successful and seemed to confirm the wisdom of moving from Melbourne. I co-ordinated a research network on sport and health with a colleague and set out to convene a physical education and sport coaching conference. The dean's wife was employed in the faculty, and it was her I had to deal with to organise and promote the conference. I got on well with the dean but not with his wife. One small problem I had to deal with was over her wanting to charge PhD students the same registration fee as fulltime academics for the conference.

"Have you ever done this before?" I asked her.

She was offended by my rhetorical question.

In the same year, a French university invited me to spend three months there as an Invited Professor to teach and do research. I was asked to arrive in April 2007 and applied to the dean for permission to go. Soon after, he asked me to meet him in a small lecture room instead of his office, which was odd. There, I was confronted by the dean and five other people. He asked me to take a seat facing them and explained to me that my leave application was too late for formal approval, but something might still be arranged.

"You've done a good job developing this program, Richard, and given it a good start, but it will need managing if you are to be away."

"I'd be happy to run it from France," I said, "but I understand if you want someone here to oversee it while I am away."

"That is what I was thinking, Richard," he replied. "It might even be a good opportunity to refresh the program with some new leadership, if you are happy to hand over the reins."

He wanted to have a member of staff who was a friend of his wife take over the program. However, with the program a roaring success, I felt there was no need to refresh it. The design and implementation of my study abroad program had been my standout success at the university, and I was reluctant to hand it over to someone who I knew could not do it justice. On the other hand, I really wanted to go to the Université de Franch Comté, so I agreed.

My expectations of what my time in France would be like were surpassed by the experience. I went one month ahead of Chiho and Amy because Amy was competing in the NSW state swimming championships. On my first night, I was the only person in the fort as I walked on a rampart high above the street outside in the cold of April. Looking out over the old city from the walkway, I was struck by the beauty of the high-pitched roofs, covered in snow. I imagined what it might have been like being a soldier in this fort during the 16th century, and as my mind drifted, I could have been in another world—or time. Back in the present, I wondered why I was so lucky.

My French was poor, but I discovered a nearby wine bar where the owner's wife was Japanese. When I needed some social interaction and wine, that is where I would head to and soon became a frequent visitor. One night after staying there later than usual, I returned to Fort Griffon to find the gates closed. I had not understood that they closed the gates at a certain time and found myself locked out. Looking up, I felt dwarfed by the massive old gates that reached far up into the clear black sky.

With no one in the fort at night my only way to get in was to scale the ten-metre-high gates. Uncomfortable with heights, I had to put my fear aside to focus on the job in front of me. I collected myself before beginning the climb and committed to not looking down. It was easy getting a grip on the timber, lattice gates and my progress was smooth until I reached the top. When I tried to swing my right leg over the top of the gate, it started to rock. Ten metres above the ground, I kept my anxiety under control and returned my right leg to where it had been on the outside of the gate after which the rocking stopped. I then did a couple deep, slow breaths. As I exhaled, I felt my body weight on my feet, and the anxiety abated. Calmed and focused, I tried again and with minimal movement of the gate, got both legs on the inside of the gate. The climb down was easy and after a hot shower, I fell asleep in the warm comfort of my bed.

I did most of my teaching at the university over the month when I was on my own and spent the rest of the time writing my first academic book on sport in the lives of young Australians and discussing research collaboration with my host, Nathalie. The first few weeks on my own were exciting, but in quiet moments I felt lonely and particularly on my own at night in Fort Griffon.

By the time Chiho and Amy arrived at Charles de Gaulle Airport, I was missing them so much that I had to hold back tears of joy when I picked them out from the crowd. We stayed in Fort Griffon, which is a 17th century fortress, listed by UNESCO as a World Heritage site and overlooking the historic city of Besançon. We lived in a 200 square metre, three-level 'apartment' in the old soldiers' quarters, above where the stables were.

Amy attended the local primary school of ninety students and four teachers with one of them Japanese. Going to a new school is a challenge for any child, but when it is in a foreign country where s/he doesn't speak the language, it is likely to be very confronting. I hadn't left Australia until I was twenty-five, and here Amy was going to school in France at ten after having been to a Japanese primary school for a few weeks at ages six and eight.

I felt her anxiety when I dropped her off and asked her to be brave, which she was. At lunch time I waited outside the school gate to pick her up for the two-hour break, as I would do five days a week over the next two months. Bursting with happiness, she ran toward me with a huge smile on her face. She loved the school, the warmth, and her freedom to decide a lot of what she would study as they took advantage of her being a native speaker for their English classes. We then walked up the cobblestone street with the smell of freshly baked bread making us both hungry as we entered a boulangerie on the way home.

"*Je voudrais une baguette et deux bonbons s'il vous plaît,*" she said.

With a warm baguette under her arm, Amy and I headed home up the hill to enjoy the two-hour lunch break in what was to become a daily ritual over the next two months.

Death on the Other Side of the World

When my application for promotion to associate professor at Sydney University was denied, I was told that I didn't have enough sole-authored journal articles. The publication of sole authored journal articles was actually my main strength in the application I submitted, so I smelled a rat, but knew there was little I could do about it.

My first few years at the University of Sydney had been like a dream come true. Everything I tried worked, but, as I accelerated and my self-belief strengthened, I seemed to make some people uncomfortable. I was also often a little too honest and direct for my own good. After my disappointment at missing out, I was not desperate but began to think about looking for a job elsewhere.

A few months later, a position for a professor working in physical education and sport coaching at a UK university caught my eye. Leeds Met was one of many modern universities in the UK that had previously been polytechnics, and the new Vice Chancellor had decided to make the university distinct by focusing on sport. He was looking to attract good researchers working in sport from across the world, and I was very interested. Jumping from senior lecturer to professor would be a big step up in my career. I applied, and Leeds Met flew me over for an interview.

Walking into the interview room, I faced a long table in a large room with six people sitting at it. Standing in front of these six people reinforced for me how important the position was. I had a view of the Leeds Rhinos rugby league ground to my left and beyond the panel was Headingly Cricket ground. My PhD supervisor headed the interview panel, which indicated the importance of the job for the faculty and university. I thought I performed well and in the interview and was upbeat about the possibility of living in Leeds.

I was at a conference in Macau when Leeds Met called me to offer me the position. I told them that I was pleased and would discuss the offer with my family. Chiho was elated when I told her. I talked with Bill about being so far away as he approached an age when he might need help, but he said Sue would look after him and, again, told me not to waste the opportunity. Moving to Japan on my own in 1990 had been a big decision, but moving my family to the UK would prove a bigger and far more complicated process.

Amy was distraught when I broke the news to her. She had exceeded my expectations in sport and academic achievement. She excelled in pool swimming at state, national and international levels and in ocean swimming, the nippers, and athletics. She had been accepted into a selective Year 5 and Year 6 Opportunity Class (OC) at Neutral Bay primary school and even won the Mosman mini marathon for primary school children.

"I have done everything you ever asked me to do in sport and at school and now you want to rip me away from my friends and my life in Sydney to go to England!"

I felt terrible, but there was no turning back now.

To add to these challenges, I made a mistake with the visa application for Chiho to prove we were married, and her application was denied. I had submitted proof from the church instead of from the government, so I had to reapply and found the British Consulate was very difficult to deal with. What I thought was a simple mistake took two months and a great deal of money to correct. I had to go to the UK on my own until Amy and Chiho could get their visas.

After selling our apartment in St Leonards, Chiho and Amy had to move into temporary accommodation as they waiting to hear from the British Embassy. From England, there was not a lot I could do. I was renting a room in Harrogate and before receiving my work mobile had to walk to a public phone late at night or early in the morning to speak to Chiho. It was very cold for me and one night someone had vomited all over the phone.

Before I arrived at Leeds Met, the Vice Chancellor resigned and departed. The grand plan that had attracted me to the job seemed like it was not going to happen. Despite this, I saw the positive side of my move. There was a good team of researchers at Leeds that, in five years' time, would take the university to number two in the UK for research on sport, and I was appointed as a professor and director of a research centre on sport and physical education. A few months later, the faculty director of research was seconded, leaving a vacancy that I successfully applied for.

Within six months, I had moved from being a senior lecturer with my options diminishing in Sydney to professor, director of a research centre and director of research in a huge faculty focused on sport. I did a lot of listening and watching in the early stages of my new position in the faculty and paid attention to how the dean, Gareth Davies, operated. Gareth was a former high profile international rugby player who had been captain of Wales and played for the British Lions. He had no previous academic leadership experience, but drew successfully on his extensive experience in business and sport. Firm yet always calm and confident, he was a good listener and communicator. He empowered his senior staff by giving them responsibility and autonomy and holding them accountable.

Yorkshire is the largest county in England and possibly the most distinctive. During the 2009 Ashes (cricket) series between Australia and England, the fourth test was played near the university at Headingly. There is no better time for a bit of sporting banter between Australians and the English, than when there is an Ashes test (cricket) series on. The first day of that test also highlighted the division in England between the north and the south for me. I spent the first day in the cheap and cheery section at the stadium that becomes more rowdy as the long day progresses and the fans drink more beer. Australian player, Peter Siddle, was fielding on the boundary in front of where I was sitting, with the crowd taking the piss out of him but he took it in his stride. He smiled at some of the of the comments and communicated with the crowd. All in good fun. When England was fielding with a player in a similar position to where Siddle had been, the banter turned to abuse.

I found this a little odd so asked the man next to me why he was abusing the England player. "Why are you giving him a hard time? He's on your team isn't he?"

"Ee's a fuckin' southerner," he retorted. "Go back to where you fuckin' come from," he shouted at the player.

Yorkshire has a rough side that is reflected in the behaviour and reputation of the infamous Leeds United (football) fans. I didn't attend any Leeds United football (soccer) games but was on a train full of their supporters going to a game once and found them extremely unpleasant. I was lucky that my wife and daughter were not with me. One other minor incident I can recount was in my senior leadership role when I had dinner at a Headingly restaurant not far from the university with a senior figure from Victoria University in Melbourne. The Aussie and I had talked more formally earlier at university and sat at a table next to the window that I had asked for. I was talking up the university and Yorkshire, when two very drunk men staggered up to where we were seated and stopped. Struggling to stay upright and oblivious to us, one put his hand up at about head height on the thick glass window. Leaning his weight on his hands and looking down at the footpath, he raised his head to projectile-vomit what looked like his dinner onto the glass in front of us. No more than 150 centimetres from where I was sitting, we had front row seats to watch in silence as his vomit slid down the glass toward the footpath. The two drunks then turned to stagger off, but before I could say anything to my guest, they returned. Turning toward the vomit, one unzipped his fly to urinated on the vomit-streaked window, which he and his mate found very funny.

"Welcome to Leeds," was all I could say to my Australian guest.

Chiho, Amy and I first lived in a small village called Pannal, which was not what I had hoped for. Not much ever happened, and we never felt accepted apart from when we went to the Black Swan pub for dinner. We moved to Leeds the following year, and Amy joined the City of Leeds swimming club to continue her growth and development as a swimmer. We also enrolled her in The Grammar School at Leeds (GSAL), which saw her move from mid-year in Year Six at Neutral Bay Primary School to the end of the first year of secondary school in England. She was soon confronted by exams in courses she knew nothing about, like British history and Latin, but the school was very helpful. The quality of teaching was better than anything she had experienced before, and the teachers were all happy to give up their free time to help her catch up. Honoring my promise to get Amy a puppy in England we bought a baby German Shepherd that she named Anton.

Amy's sporting ability helped her fit in, and, after a difficult start at school, she made friends and did very well academically at the end of the year. Getting into the top swimming squad at Leeds was very difficult because it had the only 50 metre pool in the city. The coaching approach was, 'old school' and, for those in the top squad, there were always many young swimmers waiting to get in. Amy made a lot of good friends in the swimming club and climbed up the ranks to eventually win silver and bronze medals at the British national age group championships. We spent most weekends attending carnivals and even flew home for the September 2009 Australian national schools championships in Perth where she was beaten by the slimmest margin possible for the gold medal in the 100 metre breaststroke. I was very involved in my daughter's swimming, which was well aligned with my work, and my career was progressing as well as I could have hoped for.

Amy had adjusted to the change from Sydney to Leeds. She loved studying French, German and Latin, and was very pleased with her achievements in swimming and biathlon at national level. Chiho was not yet comfortable, but slowly settling in. We were looking into buying a house. The big move from Sydney to Leeds had opened up new direction and possibilities for me, and my family, after the sadness of my loss of Greg and Mum.

Then, at a swim meet in Sheffield, I received a text on my mobile from the Byron Bay police asking me to call them, which worried me. I headed out to find a public phone because I couldn't make international calls on my work mobile.

The policemen's strong Aussie accent at the other end was comforting as he told me that "We normally do this in person, but that is obviously impossible because you are in the UK, so I have to do it by phone and I apologise for that."

As he spoke I was bracing myself for the bad news about Bill when he told me that Sue had died. I was lost for words but managed to ask "…how?" She had committed suicide with Bill's old, single shot, .22 calibre rifle, the same rifle Greg had used in the desert to shoot rabbits and which featured in so many photographs he took and pasted in his diaries.

The policeman gave me a few more details as I fought my emotions. As it happened, Sue had asked her boyfriend at the time to drive down to the nearest supermarket to buy cat food and while he was away, shot herself in the abdomen. When he returned, she asked him to take her to the hospital. She walked into the Byron Bay Hospital ER with him supporting her. He told staff at the front desk that she had shot herself, but the nurse was sceptical until Sue showed her the wound and the blood pulsing from it. The ambulance rushed her up to Tweed Heads Hospital, which is a distance of about 70 kilometres, but she died before she got there. I did not break down on the phone but as soon as I hung up I slumped against the wall of the phone booth, overwhelmed by despair and grief.

I felt like I had been winded and kicked in the guts. I was struggling to stay on my feet. I was in a phone booth in Sheffield, with little awareness of the world moving by outside, and I felt alone, powerless and disoriented.

Finally, I crossed the road to have a coffee and get control of my grief before returning to the pool. Losing Sue was a big enough shock but it was harder to deal with because of the circumstances, and I couldn't help thinking about the influence that the last time I saw her had on her decision to take her life.

It was October 17, 2010.

I immediately took leave to fly home from England. Our father had not long been in the old people's home in Suffolk Park, and there would now be two sad, empty houses. A little later, Chiho and Amy flew out from the UK to attend the funeral at the local, Ewingsdale Church that the new freeway left removed from the rest of the world. It was a beautiful and peaceful place for Sue's funeral.

The church was packed inside with about a hundred people outside in the hot sun. Sue had a diverse range of friends and, as a local musician, she associated with quite few colourful people. There was a small group of suspect looking characters across the old Pacific highway and under the beautiful fig trees, with some sitting on the bonnets of their cars. They wanted to say goodbye their own way.

Sue had surfed a bit and spent several years doing karate where she tasted success in competitions but always lost to Fairlie when she met her. Fairlie was taller, older and more confident, but Sue pushed her in every bout they had. When younger, she fearlessly charged along the beach between The Pass and main beach on Shiloh and later enjoyed ripping around town on her big Honda 500 off-road bike but it was music that helped her find herself. She played guitar, but drumming was her passion and she was a good at it. She laid the solid foundation bands need, instead of trying to flout her skills. Drumming is what she was best known for around the Bay, as the first chick drummer.

At the service, Amy read an extract from the bible inside the hall. Her private school English accent was very noticeable to me among the strong Aussie accents of most locals. Bill sat in the front row, confused due to grief and the onset of dementia. "My beautiful daughter," he said to me outside, as he touched her coffin and looked into my eyes, and I held back the tears. He lacked the sharpness and focus that I had grown up seeing in his eyes but I felt great love for him. I put my hand on his shoulder and felt him relax. I knew I had to take responsibility for seeing this through, looking after my father, the family home and the future of the Lights. I had lost three of my wonderful family and now had to look after my aging father. In one way, I was thankful for Bill's developing dementia. It shielded him from the debilitating grief and emotional pain that he did not deserve to feel again after the loss of his son and his lifelong love.

Missing her mother very much, Sue had wanted to be closer to Bill and care for him. As Betty had said when Greg died, "It's just not right for a child to die before his or her parents" and now Bill had lost two of his three children, and his wife. A little distant from his daughter over most of her life, Bill had begun to feel close to her, but now she had gone and he was on his own. For any father, this is almost unthinkable. Losing my little sister was difficult for me to deal with because the last time I saw her we had a big disagreement and parted on bad terms. I couldn't help thinking about how lonely she must have been on her own and wondered what part this might have played in her suicide. I could easily have let grief and guilt overwhelm me.

Sue was in the coffin, and my father was beside me with my thoughts oscillating between sadness at losing my sister and sorrow for my father. Flashes of Bill's importance in my life rushed through my mind. I appreciated what he had faced and achieved in his life, and I thought if could ever emulate how he dealt with his life's challenges, I would be very satisfied. He had risen from barefooted poverty on a chook farm to getting a scholarship at the most prestigious high school in NSW. He recovered from being a quadriplegic at the age of 16, survived the war, and then graduated from the University of Sydney as a teacher when it was a far more respected and well paid job than it is today. He took on the challenge of learning to surf in his forties and scored a job as English Master at Mullumbimby High School to provide a wonderful life in Byron Bay for us all. He had looked after me all my life and now it was my turn to look after him.

Sue loved her cats, and when I started cleaning up her home, I found a note on a scrap of paper that she had written not long before her death. She wanted to be cremated and have her cats cremated. She wanted her ashes buried with those of Mr Poz, her favourite cat that had recently passed away. I found homes for her cats but felt obliged to follow her wishes for her own cremation. I was uncomfortable with her ashes being separated from Greg's and Mum's but followed her wishes. She had been full of energy and enthusiasm and a very popular person among her friends but a little odd in the latter part of her life. That is when I started losing contact with her, and she seemed increasingly distant from me. She would sleep through the day and stay up until early morning to watch movies and other TV. She also smoked lots of dope—too much, I thought. Thinking back, I could see when the depression might have started to affect her, but never thought about that possibility at the time.

I wanted Sue to visit us in England when we moved there and offered to pay her air fare but she didn't want to go. Greg and I enjoyed the adventure of international travel, but not Sue. It would have been good for her and for developing a relationship between her, Chiho and Amy, but she didn't want to travel so far from home. She loved her trip across the USA with Mum but preferred to be home.

Like her two brothers, she was always up for thrills and adventure in and around Byron Bay. She sometimes jumped in the rage hole and ripped around town on a big powerful motor bike. She charged up and down the beach on Shiloh, fought successfully in karate tournaments and was a well-respected drummer in Byron Bay, but rarely left home. Apart from her USA trip, she spent short periods away in Mount Isa with Ray who was a musician boyfriend at the time, and in Sydney. She would have much preferred a cup of tea with Mum on the veranda at Ewingsdale to a coffee in a Parisian café. Jonson Street over Champs-Élysées, any day of the week.

While we were in England, Bill's doctor and people close to our family contacted me to suggest it was time for him to be looked after professionally so when the opportunity to speak to Sue face to face arose I took it. I flew to Australia for a conference and took some time off to go home and put Bill in a nursing home. Before that trip, I asked Sue by phone and Email to put him in a nursing home, but she wanted to keep caring for him. She enjoyed being close to him and getting the affection she had wanted when younger. Getting enough affection from her father when growing up with two older brothers too full of confidence was difficult, and he was now her family.

Bill had been living in our family home on his own, while Sue lived in her cottage about 20 metres away, but this arrangement didn't work because he needed someone with him. As one example, someone I knew picked him up wandering down the lane around one to two o'clock in the morning wearing nothing but his senior nappy. I wanted Sue to live in the same house and suggested she decide which house that would be and then rent the other one to generate a little income for her, but she disagreed. That convinced me that Bill would be happiest in a nursing home where he could live comfortably in safety with medical attention close at hand.

After Mum passed away, Sue had enrolled in an early childhood teacher education program. It would have been an ideal career for her, and she thought ahead about setting up a child care business at her home she was going to call 'Pebbles and Bam-Bam'. She was developing confidence and setting herself long term goals, which were both good for her. With government assistance, it all looked good for her, but she ran into problems. Bill took over to guide her through the program but got it all wrong. He had her doing units as they/he pleased instead of in the required order that would allow her to complete the course, semester by semester. Already beginning to lose his way intellectually, he steered her in the wrong direction and would not consider any questions she had about how she was progressing.

I was living in Sydney then but should have been suspicious about Bill's behaviour when he stayed with us at St Leonards. He wanted to have a swim in our pool, but, when he got in, he thrashed around for a few seconds then stopped to stand in the waist deep water and shouted, "Christ I can't bloody swim! I've forgotten how to swim."

On the same trip, we later took him to the airport for his return flight to Byron Bay. Chiho and I took him to check in and put him to the right queue with his bags, made sure he had his ticket, and said goodbye. He had so much trouble checking in that we had to go back to the airport to sort out the problem.

Sue lost her government assistance to study and withdrew from the program but picked up a job that she loved at the local IGA supermarket. She worked in the deli section and was the happiest I had seen her for a long time, which is something many other people who knew her well also thought. She had security, a regular income, daily social interaction with customers and plenty of self-esteem. Very popular and good at her job, she was a changed person. She was settling into a satisfying lifestyle and re-building her self-esteem until it was clear to her that Bill was starting to develop dementia and needed help. She wanted to look after him so quit her job at IGA to work as a carer for him with government financial assistance. She not only felt a sense of duty and obligation but also enjoyed getting closer to her father and knowing that he relied on her.

While I was home, I saw an opportunity to move Bill into the nursing home when Sue went into hospital for a major operation in Lismore. I forged her signature that I needed to have him admitted, and took him to the nursing home in Suffolk Park. It was the best thing for Bill, but, when I found out about her death, I wondered how much my actions might have influenced her decision to take her own life.

Growing up in the Bay, Sue, Greg and I had all been full of energy, drive and enthusiasm, but we ended up living very different, and separate lives. Perhaps her overt enthusiasm and energy that Greg and I also inherited made stable relationships difficult? She may have been a women before her time. Sue and I had gone in very different directions and I had no idea that she struggled with depression. I got on very well with a father of one of Amy's friends at primary school in Sydney as we were both very keen on sport and very supportive of our daughters' efforts. He was a loving father and husband but one Christmas day he drove to North Head in Sydney and jumped off the cliff to his death. With no idea he had depression, his death shocked me.

Putting Bill in the aged care home while Sue was in hospital damaged my relationship with her. I had hoped it would heal over time, but I never got to see her again. Her story is sad and things did not seem to have lined up in life for her. She came close to finding flow in her life a few times but it always evaded her in one way or another. After her death, friends told me not to blame myself, which seems to be a common reaction when people lose a loved one to suicide. Like Greg's, her death was violent and confronting for me. It was not until I went to a Melbourne clairvoyant (a birthday present from Chiho) in 2011 that I started to heal. As with the deaths of my brother and mother, I accepted the reality of her death and the pain it inflicted on me. There was no escape from the grief, and I could not bring her back, but I was able to draw on losing Greg and Mum to negotiate and accept death, and focus on the present.

Back Down Under

I had planned to develop my career in England and craft a new life for us, but Sue's sudden death sent us all home. As part of our plan to live long term in England, I had bought a beautiful German Shepherd we named Anton to honour my promise to Amy that we would get her a puppy when we moved to England. When Sue died, he was already part of the family and came with us back to Australia, but not without complications, financial cost and a great deal of damage to his mental health. We also had to bring our cats Tiger and Myshka. Tiger was a street cat from Osaka who had lived in Brisbane, Melbourne, Sydney and Leeds, then back to Sydney and Melbourne, where he died at age 20. Myshi was his young female Burmese companion that he loved and cared for. They were a great couple.

I started looking for a job in Australia but professors' positions in sport coaching, physical education or sport sociology were not common. I applied for a position at a university in Sydney after an Australian colleague and friend at Leeds Met who was well aware of my situation had urged me to go.

"Just go, Richard. Looks like you've got a job but even if you don't, someone with your profile will easily get a job back in Australia."

I paid the costs of moving my family and our pets from England to Australia, but I didn't get the job. There I was, back in Australia, stranded in Sydney, paying high rent with Amy in an expensive private school but without a job. It was a difficult time for me and the family.

While I was in the UK, I supervised an Australian staff member who undertook a part time PhD and had to send my CV to get approval from his university. When the relevant people at the University of Ballarat saw it they asked if I was interested in working there, and I had said no. Now, in very different circumstances, I contacted them to ask if the offer was still open, and fortunately it was.

Ballarat is about 120 kilometres west of the Melbourne CBD by road, but we rented a place at North Balwyn in the eastern suburbs of Melbourne. Chiho didn't want to live in Ballarat and wanted Amy to stay at the private school in Melbourne.

It is a great suburb and we were very happy there but travel to work and back was demanding for me. Each work day, I woke up at 4.30 am to get on the tram to Southern Cross railway station. I would then catch the train to Ballarat where I would wait for the bus to the university. Door to door, this took about three and a half hours, which made it seven hours a day travel. Driving was quicker but took its toll on the car and if my timing was out, traffic over the Westgate Bridge could be awful.

On a three year contract as a professorial research fellow, I had very little teaching and limited leadership responsibilities, so I only needed to go to my office three days per week, which made things easier. In 2012, the Vice Chancellor launched one of my most successful books on physical education and sport coaching pedagogy, and I maintained a high output of quality publications. Chiho, Amy and I settled back into life in Melbourne and I was very grateful for the job that the University of Ballarat gave me.

I called Bill every day at his nursing home in Byron Bay, but, over time, he started to drop the phone and wander off. Once every six weeks or so, I flew to Byron Bay to see him, sometimes with Amy. It could have been very sad for me to watch my father's intellectual and physical decline, but at least his nursing home looked after him well.

During his early days at the home, Bill danced, sang to the nurses, and flirted with them, but time slowed him. There were other patients in different stages of decline there who did and said silly things. They talked in ways that Amy and I thought were funny, and we would engage in conversations with them that amused us. We laughed with, and at, Bill and I was always happy to see him smile when he recognised us. As a teacher, he was liked for his sense of humour and it stayed with him until his last couple of years.

Between my visits, I was surprised and concerned about how quickly Bill's condition declined. A year or two, he needed a wheelchair and was soon confined to bed as the end of his life quickly approached. Amy's company was very helpful for me and the significance did not escape me. I was looking after my elderly father toward the end of his wonderful life with my young daughter helping me as she moved into her adult life.

The last time I saw Bill, he was unable to communicate even with his eyes, which were shut the whole time I was with him. He'd already lost his ability to speak. There he lay, face up with his eyes closed as memories of him flooded my mind. Him trying to teach me to tackle in the back yard, his low, wide stinkbug surfing stance, pacing up and down the Byron Bay pool as I did my early morning swimming training. Him practising his golf on the property and hobbling across the paddock as his hips deteriorated because he put off surgery. Most of all, I remembered his sense of humour, his enthusiasm and his zest for life—attitudes I think I have inherited and wanted to pass on to Amy. What more could I have asked for from my father?

"Good-bye Bill, I love you," I said, kissing him on the forehead and then walking out of the room for what was the last time.

A week later, on Father's Day, my phone rang at 5.30 am. Someone from the home told me that Bill had just passed away in his sleep. I knew it was coming, but it still hit me, and I looked down in silence for a few seconds. I felt sad that we had physically parted and that he was no longer on this earth. After thanking the person who had called me, I hung up and lay back in bed. I felt loss and emptiness, but did not cry. I thought that Bill was ready for whatever comes after death. From as far back as I can remember he had always been there and was my go-to-person. I woke Chiho up to tell her that Bill had gone.

There had been no formal funeral or ceremonies to say goodbye to Greg and Mum, but we had them for Sue and Bill because I was able to organise their funerals. Bill's was at St Paul's Anglican Church in Byron Bay. I asked Amy to read one of his favourite poems, which was 'Birches' by Robert Frost. His favourite line was: "Earth's the right place for love: I don't know where it's likely to go better."

He was a brilliant and passionate teacher who connected with young people. A sensitive man, he loved life, had a great sense of humour, and could captivate otherwise disenchanted young people like me. He could bring a book, a play, a poem or a battle in ancient Greece to life in the classroom and engage his young audience.

Though school did little for me, Bill's English literature, poetry and ancient history classes always interested me.

Someone from the Army read out his service record, talked about Bill's work in Intelligence and said that much of what he did in Darwin and Brisbane was still top secret. Bill had been sent by troop train to Darwin to be deployed in the battle against the Japanese as they approached Australia. In a lesson on setting up a mortar to hit the desired target, he watched patiently as an officer struggled to get the calculations correct. When it looked like the officer was stuck, Bill put up his hand to respectfully correct him and impressed someone enough for them to look up his details. When they saw that he had been educated at Sydney Boys' High with good grades, they pulled him out of his regiment to put him in Intelligence.

Bill was later transferred to Brisbane to work in a unit that cooperated with US Intelligence under General McArthur. When listening to Japanese 'chatter' between a plane and the base, his unit were sure there was someone very important on board. The plane that the US P38 fighter planes then shot down was carrying the Marshall Admiral of the Japanese Navy, General Yamamoto. For most people in and out of the armed forces, his death would have been cause for joy, but Bill said he was a little saddened by it. He saw Yamamoto as an intelligent man, educated in the USA, who had argued against attacking America. Bill felt that Yamamoto could have been providing some balance against the rampant militarists who had pushed Japan into war.

Bill had let me know he wanted his body cremated and to have his ashes placed in the water near the end rock at The Pass, as we did for Greg in 1989 and for Mum in 2001. I did as he had asked but couldn't paddle out to the end rock because it was already dark. His farewell was an experience that will stay with me forever. I walked out from the beach with the box of his ashes in both hands where we often walked to paddle out to The Pass for surf. I felt the warm water gently rise and fall against my legs as each tiny wave gently moved past to lap against the craggy rocks behind me as I emptied his ashes into the ocean. With the last remnants of light casting a beautiful purple hue over a calm ocean that welcomed my father, I felt in harmony with nature and a strong sense of there being a spiritual world.

"Bill would be stoked," said John Morgan, close behind me.

Bill's death had not generated the same grief in me as those of Greg, Mum and Sue because he was not suddenly and violently ripped away from me, but I still felt the loss of my father as the most important person in my life.

With my contract at Ballarat expiring, I took a position as head of the School of Sport and Physical Education at The University of Canterbury, New Zealand. The School was under performing in research, within a college that had a similar problem. It was only three years after the massive earthquakes that had hit Christchurch in 2010 and 2011, and the university and city were still badly affected.

Again, changing country and work helped me deal with grief. Being able to move after Amy's final exams helped ease the guilt involved in moving my family overseas again, but I wanted to rent a place that would make Chiho and Amy feel happy about the move. We rented a beautiful house on Scarborough Hill with fabulous coastal views and probably the most impressive house I have lived in. Living by the ocean and seeing the surf every morning on the way to work, Amy and I began regular surfing. We bought new wetsuits and braved the cold water, but not over winter because the water temperature goes down to eight degrees Celsius. We bought hoodies, booties and gloves, but I hated wearing them because I missed the sensations that I normally felt when in the ocean.

From the day we arrived, I felt that this was going to be a great stage in our lives. I was really looking forward to life by the ocean, surfing with Amy and my work as head of school. I loved the quaint little seaside village of Sumner that was five minutes' drive away from our home. Our local doctor had a surgery in a shabby looking old building that reminded me of *Doc Martin* on UK television. The surgery was laid back, local and very friendly, with every visit being a social experience. The doctor was getting on in years but had a sharp, dry sense of humour that I really enjoyed.

The Sumner village also had a classic old, picture theatre called Hollywood with gorgeous seating from another era. It did well because most of the opposition in town had been smashed by the two big earthquakes. There were a few good cafés, including one right on the beach that had good clam chowder and under cover seating outside with a great view of the ocean. I also liked the little surf shop called Stoked, where Amy and I hired long boards when the surf was light.

Living by the ocean was great, but again the drive to work for me and for Chiho to pick up Amy from university was too much, so we moved to Merryvale, much closer to the university.

Feeling lonely and isolated, Amy wanted to move back to Melbourne where she had a network of friends and, after my experience with Sue, I supported her. She transferred to the University of Melbourne and, although I paid for it, organised it all herself. She switched from science and French to a Bachelor of Arts with a major in philosophy and French. She did her last semester on exchange at Lyon 3 University, France and, in 2019, did the first semester of a Master in Business at a Grande Ecole in Lille before the Covid-19 pandemic hit. She had no problems making friends there before she had to return to the University of Melbourne, where she completed an honours degree in philosophy. We supported her financially, and she came back to Christchurch once a year to spend time with her family.

My work with athlete-centred coaching from around the time of Amy's birth influenced my parenting and encouraged me to empower her from an early age. There was a little tension between Chiho and me on this issue due to our different cultural upbringing, but, as Chiho adjusted to her new cultural environments and Amy grew up, it abated. We gave Amy increasing independence and responsibility year by year, and she responded well. My developing views about learning and my values for life began to align with my research and university teaching.

My first year as head of school (HoS) presented challenges I had expected, plus a few more. The staff profiles, in terms of research, were unimpressive. Like a coach taking over a losing team, this could have discouraged me, but I felt it offered me an opportunity to make a dramatic difference and threw myself into it. My optimism was boosted by the initial staff and college leadership attitude toward me and all was going to plan. The staff responded well to my presentation and pitch for the job and when I arrived, they all seemed very pleased to have me as head of school.

As one said to me while driving me from one campus to the other: "We were all surprised that you applied for the job, Richard. You came right out of left field."

The college leadership were also very pleased that I had taken the position. I felt valued, respected and supported. Everything was looking very good. In consultation with an advisory team I formed in my first week as head of school, I set out a plan to raise the performance of the school over the next five years. One focus was increasing enrolments in the sport coaching degree which, in one year, rose by 150%. I saw this as evidence of good leadership and an indication of how we could aim for massive increases in enrolments over the next four years. We also had immediate improvements in research output, PhD student enrolments and were going to host the school's first international conference only a year after my appointment.

I felt flushed with my success and enjoyed the weekly College presentations by heads of school because I always had such positive growth and development to report on. I had a bullishly positive attitude which was good for my self-confidence but contributed toward me not seeing the beginnings of trouble in the school. Half the staff bought into my vision for the future but the other half wanted to hang on to what was beginning to look like a more comfortable past to them.

Before I arrived, there had been tension brewing between the sport science and physical education staff. The sport science people all had PhDs and were recent appointments, while the PE people were former teachers with only one of them having a PhD and one having been at the university for 40 years. The PE people had a long history in the College and were accustomed to having more influence than they did with me as HoS. Thinking that that the programs only needed a little tweaking and polishing, they were unhappy with the extent and pace of change I was implementing, and their loss of power.

The sport coaching degree had only 36 enrolments in 2015 but reached 93 in 2016. From then, numbers continued to increase every year and moved beyond 200 in my fourth year at the university. The results of early changes were exciting, and I was elated with how quickly we were achieving our goals. By the end of my first year, the school was making rapid progress, and I was confident I could lead in achieving the goals of our five year plan to transform it, but some unhappy staff, led by the previous head of school, had approached the Pro Vice Chancellor (PVC) to express their concern.

"Richard," she told me, "you are beginning to move the school forward, but some staff are uncomfortable with how fast you are making changes. Don't you think you might be going too fast?"

"We've got momentum now and I don't want to lose it," I replied. "The direction we are moving in is clear, and I don't want to be held up by a small group of staff wanting to hang on to a failed past."

Despite being aware of growing division in the school, I didn't consider slowing the pace of change. Intoxicated with the rapid and dramatic progress, I overlooked this problem until we hosted the school's first international conference on coaching and teaching physical education. Half the staff and most of the PhD students worked diligently to make the conference a success, but the others didn't even attend the conference, which alarmed me.

While the Sport Coaching degree was growing so rapidly, the Physical Education degree was declining. It was so bad that enrolments had been below half the minimum forty required by the Academic Board for three years running, and they were dropping. I did a little research to find that this drop in demand was occurring across New Zealand, so I asked the PVC to suspend enrolments in PE. I suggested we offer an alternate pathway to PE teaching via the sport coaching degree and a professional qualification that we already had in the College.

Suspending enrolments for the physical education degree infuriated the staff who had been resisting change. They developed a plan to undermine me and paint me as public enemy number one for physical education teachers in Canterbury. A PhD student was tasked with contacting all PE teachers who had graduated from the program, asking them to flood the PVC with their opposition to the proposed changes. By this stage, it was too late to respond in any effective way, and then the union stepped into the fray. It reminded me of my father's discussions of major battles in ancient Greece and Rome as I realised I did not have enough knowledge of my enemy or of the environment for such dynamic change. After a big meeting with the staff, the PVC and representatives of the union, I was informed that I would need to "eat humble pie or step down as head of school." I chose the latter.

Up to this point in my academic career, I'd dealt with all the challenges that emerged effectively but now felt a bit of a failure.

Blinded by my enthusiasm and belief in what I was doing, I did not see this coming and had expected better support from above. The school was merged into a bigger school with the head of Sport Coaching and Physical Education role disappearing, but the changes I made remained and were later validated. Over the next eighteen months, every other university in New Zealand with a four year PE degree made similar changes. I had made the right decision, but did not take enough care in responding to the environment I was working in.

I stayed on as Chair of the Research Committee, at the invitation of the PVC, to make some big changes that boosted the college's performance over my three year term. I learned a lesson in leadership but did not feel the satisfaction I had hoped I would. After the appointment of a new PVC and head of the school that the courses on sport coaching and physical education were integrated into, I began to feel disconnected from the college and university.

I'd had quite a few conversations with renowned rugby coach, Eddie Jones in Japan and Australia about the influence of culture on coaching rugby and on athlete centred coaching. He told me that you have to know what is possible and what is not possible. As someone who coached Australia and England to Rugby World Cup finals, coached Japan to a win over South Africa in the 2015 Rugby World Cup and was an assistant coach or advisor for South Africa when they won the 2007 Rugby World Cup, he should know. I should have known as well, but did not think enough about the restrictions placed on my plans by the particular environment I was in.

I arrived at a time when feelings were still raw after the earthquakes in an unusual school with a troubled history. It was inward looking with existing tension that I stirred up by making big changes too quickly. After my emotions had settled, I reflected on what had happened and how it might have been related to my strong but probably, one dimensional self-belief with little consideration of my limitations.

All my international travel from New Zealand was via Australian cities, which provided me with opportunities to take a few days leave and drop in to Byron Bay to keep in touch. For decades, I had always gone to the Byronian Café, next to the Commonwealth

Bank in Jonson Street, until it closed down around 2017. On a Sunday morning, a group of ten or so middleaged locals sat at one of the long outdoor tables, talking over coffee. The café name had changed to Café Byron, but with it having the same tables and location, I still called it the Byronian. Whenever in the Bay, I always dropped in, walked across the road to buy a newspaper and chat with one of the two long-time local ladies working at the news agency, then back across the road for an espresso.

On one of these occasions, I talked with an old university mate of Greg's about his short term tourist accommodation business that was not far from our property. Damien had four or five small villas for short term holiday letting, and he seemed to be doing well.

"Damien, what potential do you think there is for me to do something similar at my place up the Lane?"

"Been a while since I've seen it, Ric, but I reckon it would be great. Maybe take out a few trees in the middle of the property and do some planting along the boundaries? It's big enough."

"Would you like to have a look at it?"

"I'd love to."

Checking out the property, encouraged me to think further about the possibilities. I had a look over his villas, and later Chiho, Amy and I travelled from New Zealand to stay there for a few days.

I was losing my passion as an academic and wondered whether or not it might be time for a new challenge, one that would bring me home. The idea of turning the old family home into holiday tourist accommodation began to make sense to me.

How Did I Get Here?

Regardless of where I was living, before Mum's death, I always made sure I was home for Christmas. Greg and I always considered our family and home when making plans for the future, and, as much as Greg enjoyed his life in Central Australia, he had planned to come home to look after his parents the year after he so tragically died. He loved adventure, but his mother and father always came first. From the age of eighteen onward, we were in and out of the Bay, but Sue always lived at home, or very near it.

After returning to Byron Bay in 1977, I decided to tidy up the property and started with cutting out all the lantana between the family house and the creek. I spent hours each day with a machete cutting lantana and pulling it out by its roots with the powerful smell of the rich, red volcanic soil thick around me. After bursting through the last wall of lantana, I had a great view of the creek. I stood there, feeling satisfied with my effort and marvelling at what seemed like a secret and magical place I had discovered.

I soon imagined living where I was standing and thought about building a little studio where I stood. I knew very little about building, but after talking with Bill and karate students of mine who had building experience, I decided to do it. With no power and using 100 year old hardwood timber that I bought in Kyogle for the frame, it was hard and hot work, and halfway through the project a freak storm smashed it to the ground. One of my karate students rebuilt it for me. Clad in 'hippy board' that was treated with engine oil, it was aptly called 'the humpy.'

Greg had cleared his part of the property for his return home, but, as one of his mates said, "the Simpson Desert got him." Sue's boyfriend at the time built a house for her where Greg had planned to build his which gave us three dwellings on the property but, by the time of Sue's death, they were all in need of some love.

Cleaning out and tidying up the family home and Sue's house was emotionally draining, but it encouraged me to reflect on my life and my family. With Bill in the nursing home and Chiho and

Amy back in Leeds, I was on my own most of the time. Sorting through report cards from primary school and old photos of my family brought back happy memories, but with some sadness because they reminded me of what I had lost.

Working in and around the old family home for several days, I had to decide what to keep and what to throw out. My mood oscillated between being lonely and feeling very connected with my family, until I discovered a box of .22 calibre bullets, with only one missing. This hit me hard, as I imagined Sue's hands on the box and her selecting the one bullet that would end her life. I also thought about the state she was in when she shot herself, and what might have been going through her head when she pulled the trigger. I felt guilt, but refused to be dragged down by it and put the box of bullets aside. The next day, I took it down to the Byron Bay Police station to hand it in.

There was my life in front of me with old photographs, hand written letters, drawings from our childhood, school exercise books and report cards taking me back in time to relive so many moments in my life. Among the smells of yellowing old newspapers, school reports and books, I was lost between the past and the present. With only the occasional car passing by on McGettigan's Lane, among the songs of familiar birds and the stillness, I reflected on my life.

Animals, nature and wildlife had always been important for me and for all my family, but the shock of Sue's death and the deep reflection that followed, brought my feelings and beliefs to the surface. She loved animals and even though she had little money, donated regularly to charities that supported animals and mostly to those trying to stop the cruel practice of extracting bile from bears, and saving them. Her death helped me recognise the importance nature held for me.

While I was living in New Zealand, the awful Australian bushfires of 2019 and political denial of its links to climate change shocked me and started me looking for answers. Reading about the Māori concept of *maramataka* helped me locate these problems in our Western relationship with nature and our separation from it. The number of people killed, the houses destroyed and the three billion animals that perished or were displaced made the 2019 bushfires the worst in Australia's modern history and clearly linked to human action. The bushfires and floods around the world were caused by an existential threat to life on earth that originates in the breakdown of our relationships with nature

Reading about *maramataka* in a Christchurch newspaper stimulated my interest enough to do some further reading. It is based on understanding the environment Māori live in and their ability to adapt to changes for survival and good health. The concept refers to knowing nature in a practical way that involves understanding how we are part of it, and its rhythms. This, and similar concepts used by other Indigenous peoples, emphasised for me how divorced from nature we have become.

In an interview with Stephanie Dowrick, Senior Australian of the year, Miriam-Rose Ungunmerr-Bauman suggested how Aboriginal belief in the importance of belonging extends to humans belonging into nature. Dowrick herself suggests that this awareness and connection with nature allows us to see how:

> ...the exploitation of the earth and the climate crisis we now recognise are symptoms of a crippling disconnection: a spiritual crisis that's inescapable and may be fatal.

Like many others during the Coronavirus pandemic in 2020, I got to know our backyard well. I would sit on the deck with Chiho every morning watching and listening to the many small chirping birds that on a few occasions included the calming fantail bird (*piwakawaka*) moving softly in front of my face. We also studied the behaviour of bees and particularly around the flowers Chiho planted and nurtured using *reiki*. She also brought bees that seemed to be dead or dying back to life, or consciousness, with *reiki*. They would recover and fly off. This strengthened my belief in the spiritual world and in the Japanese *reiki* notion of being able to channel the universe's energy into living things for them to heal themselves.

On a trip to Wellington with Chiho, I had a powerful experience of connecting with nature that further strengthened my belief in a spiritual world. Chiho and I spent two hours walking around the ecosystem, Zealandia, that protects native wildlife from introduced predators. While crossing a footbridge, we stopped to take in the view and feel the environment. I raised my hands with palms out to see if I could feel any energy and, after about five seconds, the wind picked up. I noticed this and waited another ten seconds before lowering my hands for it to stop immediately. I looked at Chiho, and she was already looking at me:

"Did you see that?" she asked. "The wind blew when you had your hands up and stopped when you lowered them."

"Yes, I saw it. Was it just a coincidence?"

"I don't know. Put your hands up again."

I was as curious as Chiho was, so I put my hands up again and within five seconds the wind blew. I held my hands up for about a minute then dropped them, and the wind stopped. We were both quietly stunned.

"*Sugoi!*" she said excitedly. "You are connecting with the wind. You raise your hands, and it blows but stops when you lower them. *Sugoi!*"

"Should I try it again? Just to make sure it is not just some kind of coincidence?"

"Yes, let's do it!"

It happened again, and we were both amazed. Stuck for words, we just walked on. I can't explain it, but I had had some sort of meaningful interaction with the spirits of nature.

My experience at Zealandia and growing knowledge of nature, energy and the spiritual world led me to realise how surfing was an activity that connected me with nature. In 1966, I found myself in an amazing natural world that I connected most with through surfing. Riding waves involves feeling, finding and connecting with energy as practical interaction with nature. Waves carry energy from deep in the ocean as swells and, as they move into shallow water, they begin to stand up until they finally break and fold forward to release their energy. Like any surfer, I understood the ocean and the conditions that created good waves when growing up at The Pass. Understanding where the wind was coming from and how strong it was, what direction the swell was coming from and how big it was meant I knew when and where the best surf would be, but I never thought about it as connecting with nature.

Greg's involvement with Indigenous Australians and my research on Indigenous sport stimulated my interest in indigenous relationship with nature. My growing understanding helped me understand how Indigenous peoples tend to have better connections with nature and ways of understanding it than people in Western societies and cultures. For example, the Australian Aboriginal concept of *dadirri* provides guidance for listening and belonging to nature. It refers to inner listening and still awareness as a way of gaining a deep understanding of nature through reflection and contemplation. In Hawaii, Indigenous connection with the natural environment includes knowing that when a certain type of crab comes to the surface, there may be an earthquake or volcanic eruption. Human relationships with nature are central to Indigenous cultures and to some Eastern religions like Shinto, which I have become interested in. It is an Indigenous and very localised Japanese religion that is essentially a sense of nature, a way of seeing and feeling nature. It acknowledges nature's spiritual powers and, although my knowledge of it is limited, it provided an explanation of my experience at Zealandia for me.

It is really only in the past decade or so when I have come to recognise the importance of nature to me. Over that time, I have also developed a critical view of how so many people see nature as a resource to be consumed and condone its mass destruction. Photos and footage of koala habitats destroyed for profit not long after the deaths of so many of them during the Australian bushfires in 2019 angered me. The unrelenting destruction of this endangered species unique to Australia and their habitat, driven by the lust for power and greed, infuriates me. Seeing koalas wandering about lost and homeless after their homes have been destroyed by developers tugs at my heart. I have the same feelings about the beautiful, humanlike orangutans in Borneo and Sumatra. The love and care the mother shows her baby is no different to a human. A video I saw of a male orangutan fighting to his death against a machine ripping up the forest and his home brought tears to my eyes. It stirred up anger and frustration at my inability to do anything.

As I cleaned out the family home in 2010, the postie delivered a letter addressed to Bill Light from Lester Brien, a former student of his at Manly Boys High (MBH) and a barrister in Sydney. He and "a few of the boys" had been talking about how much they enjoyed Bill's teaching and the positive influence that he had on them. They all liked and respected him and wanted to know how he was doing, but by that time he was unable to read, or even understand even if I had read the letter to him. Still, 40 years after Bill had left MBH, it made me think about the potential teachers have to influence young people's lives in very positive ways.

After reading the letter, I sat on the front steps in the afternoon sun as the shadows of the big camphor laurel trees retreated beyond my feet. I started to think about how important teaching was but how much its status as a profession had declined. I reflected on how much satisfaction I felt from the positive influence I had on children at primary school and high school students like the high school students in Japan that I took on a rugby tour to Australia.

A decade later I was contacted through email by a couple of students from the Japanese high school rugby team that played against Byron Bay High. They had become doctors and wanted to thank me for the experience and what they learned from me. I probably had more influence on university students in Australia, Japan, England and New Zealand, encouraging them to think about who they are, who they want to become and how they could contribute to a better society.

I thought about how happy Bill must have felt when I finally exercised my intellectual ability. I had kept chipping away at upgrading my tertiary qualifications but was not really engaged in any study until I did my masters in Japan. At that time, and married to a Japanese woman, I was hungry for knowledge about Japan and what was going on around me. I developed a voracious appetite for knowledge about its history, culture and society. During my masters research, I was able to meet the intellectual challenges involved and develop a good understanding of an environment that had puzzled me. Doing a PhD back in Australia accelerated my intellectual growth after Greg's death.

The development of flow in my life has been like a winding creek with fast flowing sections, pockets of swirling water, and some partial blockages that I have had to negotiate. Australian artist, the late John Olsen, describes these blockages as spending time in a billabong. My experience of flow has involved identifying the faster moving water and being aware of the opportunities that even disasters like family deaths can generate. It has also involved increasing inner awareness and the confidence to let my soul guide me in a non-conscious way, based on feeling and intuition rather than logic. At times, I have also needed enough confidence in my ability to take the plunge and go with the flow. With a conscious understanding of flow, I now consider it when making important decisions but it also guides me at a non-conscious level and is tied into my belief that most things in my life have happened for a reason.

Chiho's birthday, her mother's, Amy's, mine, and our wedding anniversary, are all on the 11th, which suggests something spiritual to me. Starting an academic career in the first weeks of the 21st century to retire after 21 years and arrive back in Australia on 21/1/21 are other coincidences that might have some spiritual significance. This growing awareness of life's spiritual dimension and the narrowing of the space between the physical and spiritual has helped me deal with grief.

Over my last couple of years in New Zealand, the flow of my life slowed, and that is one reason why I left. The other reason was the generous pay-out offered to me by the university to retire that, after some anxiety, pointed me in a new and meaningful direction. Chiho had enjoyed life in New Zealand and felt secure there but when discussing the offer she said to me:

"Well, if you think about it you have followed flow in your life and it has worked out for you. I know you want to go home and this seems like the flow in your life to me. I am happy here, but if we are going back to Australia, this is it."

Over my last year or two at the University of Canterbury my career plateaued to become just work. The new vice chancellor was inspiring and recognised my contribution to the university, but the gap between her and my work was too big. My international academic networks helped a lot but my immediate environment was frustrating and began to dull me.

It reminded me of what a colleague at the University Sydney said about me quitting to go to England. "Richard, when you left, PE just stalled here. We were on a roll with you here, but it just stopped. You should have stayed. We should have found a way to harness your energy."

In New Zealand, I had to deal with too many petty issues of no real significance for me or the university. I had never thought about retiring, and Chiho was shocked when a colleague asked her when I would retire. I had not thought about what comes next after retiring, but now I had a plan for my post academic life that energised me and gave me strong direction.

Despite the deaths in my family, I developed an overall, happy disposition and a positive, grounded attitude. As an academic, I read about, and worked with psychological and sociological theories on what makes people happy and promotes wellbeing. This got me thinking about how and why I was generally happy, positive and calm, and what I could do to further develop or at least sustain, my wellbeing.

For me, the most important factor contributing to this is leading a life, and having work, that has meaning. My academic career and the more recent project of establishing an accommodation business in Ewingsdale by restoring the family home had deep meaning for me. They both created meaningful challenges that motivated me and keep me busy. The most recent stage of turning over the family home to short term accommodation has been very demanding during a demanding economic environment, but the meaning it has for me is very motivating.

The old 'Humpy' is now a cute little 'Villa' that is very popular, and we have opened the family home for guests who all love it and feel its energy. Both houses have positive energy with tenants and guests typically happy and feeling good. Feeling happiness and dealing with grief has often involved an element of what could be seen as good luck, or perhaps it was part of the flow of my life. These included being offered a rugby coaching job in Osaka so soon after Greg's death, and getting a job so quickly after returning to Australia from the UK.

My experiences of grief have led me to accept that death is a fact of life that affects, and awaits us all. It has even been suggested that, without human suffering and death, life is not complete. The first three deaths in my family were all-consuming as I battled against grief and the huge holes it created in my life, but each time I grew a little. When Greg, Mum and Sue died, I fell and had to fight to get back to where I had been in my life, but it was part of an overall, upward life trajectory.

Dealing with each death made me think about the big questions, like why am I here? what is the purpose of life? And what happens after death? Each death encouraged me to think about what it is to exist and how there must be so much more to being than just our physical existence. I came to realise that although I lost four people I loved very much it was only in a physical sense, and I can still love them.

The sudden and shocking loss of Greg and Sue was awful, but I began to focus on my spiritual connections with them. For each of the four deaths, the sadness that I felt about my physical loss provided a deep connection with them and a sense of their presence as I re-experienced moments spent with them and dialogue between us. Since Greg's death, there has not always been a clear division between happiness and sadness for me and, as painful as it has been, I can now look at grief as a positive experience. Grief intensified my love for my family through reliving and valuing positive, past experiences with them. As Leventhal suggests, death can promote deep reflection on our place in the world and lead to a new level of consciousness. From a positive psychological perspective, this 'post-traumatic growth' reinforces the idea that suffering transforms us.

Since Greg's death, difficult times and tough challenges for me have invariably been accompanied by opportunities. When Greg was killed, it was the lowest point in my life. My spirit plummeted and I was unable to make sense of it. Why? Why? I asked myself. I don't have the answer, but I came to accept his death and remain connected to him in ways other than the physical. This acceptance of death has been the key to dealing with grief for me and letting it become an experience that positively shaped my growth.

I think that we place too much importance on the physical aspects of life and far too little on its spiritual aspects. I have a photo of Greg and me on my bedside table that I look at when I go to bed and get up. Photos of the others in my family I have lost are also in a place in our home where I see and think of them many times a day. After Greg's death, the opportunity to be a professional rugby coach in Japan helped me accept what happened, focus on the present, and then work toward setting and realising long term goals. This valuable learning formed a turning point that sent me in a different direction.

Since Greg's death, I have come to accept what can't be changed but learned not to shy from meaningful challenges and underestimate myself. In my early twenties, I quit a secure job that I enjoyed to get my black belt in Hong Kong and teach karate in my hometown. Not long later, I lay on a bed of nails for the first time and took on working as a professional rugby coach in Japan with not so much relevant experience. Getting a PhD in my forties and then pursuing a successful career as an academic might not be particularly impressive, but it reflects significant growth for me. Expelled from Year 12 and shown the door in my first semester of teachers' college, I felt a strong sense of achievement when awarded a PhD at the University of Queensland in front of my mother, father, wife and daughter. Leaving Sydney, where Chiho and I had bought a beautiful new apartment in St Leonards, for Leeds was risky, and three years later, our chaotic return to Australia, with all its complications after Sue's death was confronting. These and other achievements are not as important as my continuing internal development, and not what people see or think about them.

When I took acid and drank magic mushy coffee as a young man, I was not consciously looking for enlightenment but was influenced by the counter culture discourse up to the late seventies. Part of this was the belief that Eastern views of life and practices like meditation could enlighten people and free them from disenchantment with their world. I think this predisposed me toward the philosophy underpinning Japanese martial arts that has had a big influence on my development. It also seems to have shaped my core beliefs that have stayed with me.

Traditional Japanese martial arts as training for life is reflected in the term *būdo*, which means the martial way/path. It sees youth as an important stage of life's journey that is full of opportunities for learning and not the destination. From this perspective, life learning is spiritual, moral and personal development achieved through physical experience. It is internal development that occurred more through physical experience than I was aware of at the time.

The concept of life-long learning makes sense to me as does John Dewey's idea of learning through a lifelong continuum of experience but they sit in contrast to the contemporary emphasis on immediacy and the appearance of the body with youth as the pinnacle of life. Over the last decade or so, I have grown internally with my perspective on life influenced by the Japanese concept of *wabi-sabi* that encourages me to accept the journey of life and enjoy *all* of it.

This notion is well captured by the late Australian artist, John Olsen:

It's all in the search, the constant looking, staying fully alert and alive. It's not about achieving success. There are people who are very successful, but live bastards of lives, nothing makes them happy, because their goal of success is what matters, not the searching journey to reach it. To me, the journey is it, not the arrival.

To finish this chapter, I draw on a Japanese TV show called *Hajimete no Ostukai* (*My First Errand*) in Japan. The series was called *Old Enough* when shown on Netflix in 2022 and was reported on in one of the Sydney newspapers (Mitchell, 2022, April 27). Following the adventures of Japanese toddlers who are given the responsibility of running errands on their own, it shows how they dealt with the challenges and stress involved. The journalist identified what he felt are valuable learning experiences for any adults watching the program. He suggested what we can learn from watching toddlers tackle such tasks for the first time and how it can remind us of the extent to which we underestimate what we are capable of doing. This resonates with my experiences of becoming who I am and what I have learned from the journey so far.

From dealing with grief and lying on a bed of nails to getting my PhD and developing a successful career as an academic, I have exceeded my own expectations and not just from an external perspective. In what John Olson refers to as the third act in life I have come to value, be aware of and develop my internal and spiritual capacity. Below I list and comment on what Mitchell suggests are the three main life lessons we can all pick up from this show because of their relevance to my story:

Challenge yourself and find out how much more you are capable of achieving than think you are.

This is demonstrated in the show by a toddler who breaks down in tears but, after some kind words of encouragement from a grandparent, succeeds in completing the task. For me, this has typically involved overcoming fear, self-doubt and anxiety that is linked to self-awareness while having the drive, belief and desire to do my best, with motivation coming from within.

Never ever give up.

This is recognition of how quickly we take the easy way out by giving up which is easy and convenient. I think the idea of never giving up is a little unrealistic but does emphasise how much we need to commit to and stick with the task in front of us when the goal is worthy of the effort and risk.

Walk, don't run.

As Mitchell notes, our fast paced world and culture of immediacy is unhealthy. It places an emphasis on everything being done and available instantly while encouraging a superficial perception of success and achievement. It discourages us from setting long term goals that we work toward with patience, determination and commitment.

This is something that I now notice when teaching karate to young people after such a long break. Like so much in life, short term achievement in martial arts is typically superficial and does not compare in value to the benefits of the long haul and the internal development that comes with it.

Full Circle

Woken by the raucous calls of kookaburras before dawn, I lay in bed, soaking up each of the following outbursts. Nothing could have made me feel more at home.

Around the middle of 2020, I didn't think I would get back home from New Zealand for another year or two, but in January 2021 found myself on the family property, living in the Villa with Chiho and our cat Morgan. For an academic career that started in the first month of the 21st century coming home at the end of 21 years on 21/1/21 seemed a good omen to both of us.

At seven o'clock the next morning, I drove to IGA (a small supermarket) in the Arts and Industry Estate to buy something for breakfast, with papaya and mangos top of my list. Back at the Villa, I stood on the deck, enjoying the view down to the creek and feeling the ground under my feet. Two days later, I visited the past by parking at Captain Cook Lookout to do the same walk Greg and I had done when we first set foot on Clarkes beach. The sandy track that we charged down in 1966 had been replaced by a concrete path and steps that I walked down while taking in what was around me. The banksia trees and the sounds of the birds were familiar but, as I stepped onto the beach, the sand didn't squeak because of the heavy traffic that had churned it up over the peak tourist season.

Despite the decades that had passed, the walk to The Pass was not much different for me. The first time Greg and I hit the beach, we did not consciously take in much of what was around us as we sprinted toward The Pass, but this time I was much more aware. I felt the wet, hard sand under my feet near the water's edge and the warm water washing up my ankles and calves as each small wave completed its long journey on the white sand of Byron Bay. The sounds and smell of the waves breaking and the expansive ocean under a huge blue sky with nature all around me was intoxicating. I'm home, I thought.

The driftwood scattered along the beach, and the cunjevoi

ripped off the reefs by the recent big seas took me back to the strong cyclones that hit the Bay over the late sixties. Greg and I would walk along the beach looking for interesting things that had washed up. Our best find was the arse-end of a surfboat, but we were most excited by the possibility of finding ambergris, which is a highly valuable substance produced by male sperm whales after eating squid, and used in the production of perfume. We never actually saw or touched any but, somehow, thought we knew what we were looking for.

Knee deep in the soft, warm water at The Pass, I thought back to when I released my father's ashes into the ocean. Enveloped by an unforgettably beautiful purple hue with the light dissipating as the sun sank behind the distant hills, I felt great harmony with nature. Looking down at the end rock from The Pass, I connected with the spirits of my family. I closed my eyes for a minute to be sitting on my board at the end rock with Greg.

Back on the property, the warbling of magpies abated as night approached, and I listened to the gentle hum of insects and frogs croaking in the distance. That was until another sudden and powerful outburst from the kookaburras, followed by silence. An hour later, they shattered the calm of night to close out the day.

In the very early hours of Australia Day, 2021, Chiho and I were woken by the sounds of a male koala grunting loudly in one of the nearby gumtrees. Talking with a neighbour who has wildlife cameras on his property made me realise that the big male koala is a local and much loved. We had seen him while staying in the Villa on a trip home when living in New Zealand and just a few days before Christmas 2021, when a small, female koala rescued from McGettigan's Lane was released on our property.

The first few weeks back at home led me to reflect on a significant increase in my awareness of nature since I last lived there. Whether it is on the beach or on our property in McGettigan's Lane, nature here is dynamic, with a powerful energy and presence that keeps me alert and tuned in. Reconnecting with the natural environment of the Bay over my first week back was what most struck me about coming home, and I felt a stronger and fuller connection to my soul.

From theorising, reading, lecturing, and disseminating my knowledge of sport coaching, physical education teaching and leadership, I returned to get my hands dirty and reconnect with the land. Instead of having to decide what suit and tie to wear for a meeting or presentation, I was sweating in the hot sun in boots, shorts, a sweat-soaked old T-shirt, and a broad brimmed hat.

Feasting on half a papaya during a break, I watched the big male water dragon we call Charlie feed on insects. He and his family live under the shed and have been there for as long as I can remember. Charlie would run away when I approached him but, after a few weeks, would stop when he heard me shout "Charlie!" We would see him holding a pose near the corner of the shed, waiting patiently until he scored a bite to eat at the expense of an unsuspecting insect.

"I can't believe what I am doing," Chiho said to me, with a hint of stress. "This so different to how I have lived for so long."

"Yes, it's a long way from our little garden in Carrington Street," I replied. "It's very different, but you'll adapt to it."

"The environment is scary and threatening," she went on, scooping out the last morsel of orange flesh left in her papaya. "Even the birds are big and noisy. I'm not comfortable here."

It had been a sudden and radical change in lifestyle for her that I did not fully appreciate.

The next day I heard her screaming from the bathroom and ran to her assistance. "*Kaeru*," she shouted, pointing to the toilet. A glistening green tree frog looked up innocently at me with eyes wide open, as if to say, "What?"

Chiho slowly got used to her new environment but still felt displaced. Within the first month, she could be calm when she saw a big huntsman (spider) and just ask me to catch it. She was beginning to adapt to the powerful natural environment around her, but her first encounter with a snake was too much, too soon. On our way out, she was standing on the deck, waiting for me to lock the door when she thought she saw something moving through the fishbone ferns about ten metres away. Her knees gave way a little as she realised what she was looking at.

"Oh, my God" she said softly, "what is that?"

"A python," I replied. "It's a big one, but it won't hurt you."

"It makes me feel sick," she said, anxiously. "It moves through the ferns without moving any of them. How can it do that...where is it now?"

"Relax. It won't hurt you, but I'll call Artemis. Just stay here."

I phoned our neighbour who rescues native animals and is very experienced with snakes. She loves pythons and, every time I visit her, she always has one or two in her house that she is healing.

She came over quickly with a hessian bag. As soon as she located it, she began speaking to her gently.

"I have a feeling it's female," I said. "Am I right?"

"Yes, she is, Richard."

"How do you know?"

"Intuition."

After distracting 'Lilley', Artemis grasped her behind her head with one hand and held her body in the other. She then asked me to open the bag so she could gently place Lilly in it. Once inside, Lilley did not move at all. Artemis stroked her gently and continued to speak softly to her.

"Richard, I'll take her away for Chiho's benefit but still release her in this area. This is where she belongs. They are gentle creatures and would never hurt a human."

After putting the python in her car, Artemis then briefly explained to Chiho how gentle they are.

Chiho worked with me outside, shovelling gravel, digging, cutting, sweating, and filling gaps inside the house. This was a big change for her from gently snipping plants in the front yard of a suburban home in Christchurch.

After we moved into the middle house, a pair of kookaburras put a youngster on display for us. Bigger than its parents and very fluffy, it sat on the branch outside our bedroom window for hours practising its laugh. We named him (we guessed it was male) Kevin and took pleasure in talking to him and hearing him improve his laughing until he was able to perform like his parents. Each year since we came home, there has been a young kookaburra learning to laugh in the same tree branch that is popular with many other birds. Our family of magpies sit on the railing of the deck and sing for a few oats and, when we feed them, seem to celebrate in song. They are very intelligent, look me in the eye, talk to me and know me well. They have a photographic memory of people's faces and have over 30 complex melodies. When we first moved in, the magpie parents called their two young ones down from their tree to meet us and forage in the area out in front. Later, what we assume to be a pair of older siblings started visiting as well. Two years later, the cast changed again. We had four new black and white friends until the young male was chased off to find his own territory.

I am feeling the energy of the land and developing a stronger spiritual connection with the nature around us. We have flighty pee wees, honeyeaters and currawongs dropping in for some oats and showing their young ones what to do. We are careful not to overfeed them, and the magpies spend most of their day eating things that move and squirm in the grass.

Last year, I heard a loud thump that I thought might have come from a branch falling on the roof and went outside to see what caused it. A beautiful male Blue-faced Honeyeater had smashed into a window and lay motionless on the ground. As I gently picked him up, there was no sign of life in his limp body. Holding him in both hands, though, I felt warmth in his body as I walked around to the deck on the other side of the house and called Chiho. I wanted him to be alive and channelled my energy into his body as best I could.

As I waited for Chiho to come out, I felt him begin to move. I spoke to him calmly, and, as he regained consciousness, he looked me in the eye without even a hint of panic. I gently put him on the railing where he stood looking at me for about twenty seconds then flew to the popular tree branch about 10-15 metres away. After a minute or so, he flew off. I felt elated that he was alive and well but don't know how much influence I had on his recovery, apart from picking him up and holding him until he recovered. What I do know is how aware I was of my energy and his when he regained consciousness, and the connection I had made with this one bird. He is also now the only honeyeater that comes onto our railing to eat oats and calls me for food like the magpies.

As well as local wildlife, we had a couple of beautiful chooks who mysteriously turned up every day at our house and the Villa then disappeared by the end of the day. Sadly, one was killed by a vicious, off-the-lead dog in Taylors Lane. The remaining chook occasionally visited us with a couple of its offspring but was attacked by the alpha male bush turkey, so one of us had to walk her to the fence to go home when he was around. The chook stopped coming up, but her two offspring became regular visitors until again, one was killed by an off-leash dog. Only the kookaburras are not interested in the oats we put on the railing. The bush turkeys eat anything and are bullies among the birds. I would not hurt them but do chase them off our deck so the other birds can have a few oats.

Being back home provides a measure for me of how I have changed. I returned regularly when living in Brisbane, Melbourne, Sydney, and overseas in Japan, the UK, and New Zealand but, before returning in January 2021, had not lived in Byron Bay since 1990. I stayed in contact with friends through these visits and on social media as well as returning for deaths in my family but, during my last couple of years in New Zealand, I felt that it was time to come home. After meeting the challenges linked to Covid-19, extreme flooding and the rising cost of living, and, with Chiho beginning to adapt to life in Ewingsdale, I began to feel some flow in my life again.

The neighbours we had in Lighthouse Road have long gone and so have their homes. Our old home was also demolished and replaced by expensive apartments facing north, but the two huge Norfolk Pines my father planted on the nature strip in 1966 are still there. Our neighbours on either side moved out long ago to escape a town that had changed so much that it felt foreign to them. Most of the locals who were born in Byron Bay, went to school or settled here in the seventies and eighties, resent the influx of money, the greed and the Bay's commercialisation. They don't like the flood of movie stars, influencers and the uber rich "wankers in Range Rovers" moving in. They pine for a simple and honest past when the town was laid back and they knew everyone they saw in Jonson Street, and in the water. The surfers of the 1960s and even a couple in the late 1950s, discovered a real surfers' paradise and my family caught the tail end of it. The surf and beaches made the Bay famous among surfers, but the town itself was just a rough industrial town sustained by industries of death for many decades.

The natural beauty of Byron Bay is a huge attraction for tourists and people moving into the area. So is its still relatively laidback lifestyle and energy, but the median price of houses is now over $3 million. Before I came home in 2021, friends warned me how much Byron Bay had changed, and how it was no longer the place that we had all grown-up in. So many old locals and some far more recent locals decry the decline of the Byron Bay they knew. Even people who have been here only a couple of years tell me it's not like it used to be and no one can deny this. I am beginning to dislike the people who move in with money and no care for, or sensitivity to, the natural magic of this place. Still feeling the strength of the natural energy here, I am grateful to have the family property and feel an obligation to Greg, Betty, Sue, and Bill, and the land under my feet to protect it and the wildlife on it.

There are certainly aspects of change in and around Byron Bay that concern me, but so much of what shaped me as a person growing up in the Bay is still here. It is harder to catch a wave in summer at The Pass, but the beauty of the ocean, beaches and coastal environment are the same as when my family arrived in 1966.

In late November 2021, I received an email from Nature Conservancy Australia asking:

> …have you ever had a dream? A dream where we live in a place full of amazing creatures, stunning landscapes, and epic oceans? Where all our amazing animals are thriving, our waters are teaming with life and our people are fulfilled?"

As I read it, I thought to myself that this was close to my life in my first year at home.

Over my first winter home, I had three to four dawn surfs a week and, as I found my feet, was able to tap into the energy and rhythm of the ocean with the high I got from some of those surfs lasting for hours. It took a lot of concentration to take off on fast breaking and powerful waves at The Pass after such a long break, but a couple of waves I rode took me back to the sixties and early seventies. Waiting for a wave at the end rock and thinking of Greg was as good as I had hoped it would be, and I think he might have tossed up a couple of good waves for me.

At the beginning of 2023, good swell and constant, light offshore winds created nice smooth waves that I thoroughly enjoyed surfing with Amy. I did not surf well at all, but that didn't matter because surfing with my daughter was enjoyable enough. It took me back to surfing with Greg. After our surf, Amy and I had a little body surf in close at Clarke's. We were both lost in the sensuous pleasure of being in the water, feeling the gentle energy of tiny waves washing up on the sand and the beautiful natural environment around us.

Martial arts, and particularly karate, have been a big part of my life. My introduction to karate in 1974 was my first small step toward finding meaning and purpose in life. As I continued with it, awareness of my inner being grew and changed me. My career as an academic reduced the time I had for martial arts, but I stayed in touch and one of my aims after moving home in 2021 was to teach karate again and pass on what I had learned since the last time I taught in Byron Bay.

Not wanting to take the highly commercial road needed to make a successful business of it, I opted to teach from the heart in what I consider to be a traditional approach. I began like I did forty years before with cash payments and word of mouth as well as a few stories in local social media but without much success in attracting students. When a brown belt made a comeback to karate by joining my club, he set up a website for me that attracted a few students to my Jin Wu Koon Karate club. I don't have a big club, but the positive energy established by the students training with me attracts the right people to the *dojo*. People with different expectations don't stay beyond their first free lesson. I have a lot to share with adults and young people and get great pleasure from teaching karate the way I want to. Over 2023, I ran a couple of one-day seminars on a Saturday at the *dojo*. We finished with pizza for lunch out on the grass in front of the hall in the gentle sun. The upbeat mood, conversations and laughing shared between the mix of adults, young karate students, parents and grandparents created a wonderful sense of community.

The way I teach karate now helps my students develop as people, know themselves and move toward realising their potential. In my youth karate class, I see children and young people develop self-awareness and quiet self-confidence, and learn to focus on the task at hand. Initially unable to focus for more than 10 seconds, they develop over a few months to become grounded, more aware of themselves and able to take on challenges. They grow before my eyes and those who stay long enough change dramatically. Over 2022 and 2023, new students came and went, but a core of young *karateka* stayed long enough to develop their karate. The precision of their *kata* at gradings was a joy to watch and those who have since dropped out have probably learned enough to shape or influence their lives in a positive way. Those who stay with it will continue to grow in a positive way and those who want to are now beginning to compete in karate tournaments.

I wanted to teach karate for the pleasure of helping people develop through it, regardless of their age, and enjoy making a difference in people's lives. I offer a couple of classes two days a week for young people and adults. When I began in late 2021, classes were small, but I was happy to focus on establishing and maintaining a positive culture in the *dojo* for future students. I enjoy the energy developed from young student during class after bowing at the door with a big *konichi wa* and their calmness after meditation at the end of the class when they bow at the door on their way out while saying *arigato gozaimashita*.

My re-engagement in karate extended to attending a seminar in Osaka as part of the Hyashi Ha Shito Ryu Kai Karate 50-year celebrations in December 2022. I loved the hours I spent in Hashimoto Sensei's *dojo* and his laidback approach to teaching, or helping people learn. As always, I was very happy with how much I learned, my reconnection with his teaching and philosophy. And his presence.

At the University of Sydney, I fly down to do some heavy loads of block teaching and field trips during semester, which can be hard work, but the positive influence I am having on young adults soon to become teachers is very satisfying, and so is the dialogue between individual students and me on current issues in sport. This extends to working with international students who enrol in the course on sport and learning in Australian culture that I established at the university in 2006. It gives me a chance to develop critical, thoughtful, and independent thinkers who can debate important issues with honesty and respect for views that do not align with theirs yet express their own views. Here, I am working as Professor Emeritus and an experienced researcher in movement and learning, but it is not so different to so many of my ideas and views on teaching and learning in my first years as a primary school teacher.

My university students' enjoyment and gratitude for how I shape their learning is very pleasing as are some of the great field trips I work on. Possibly my favourite field trip is a three to four hour walk from the Spit Bridge to Manly that focuses on human relationships with nature as a response to the rapidly growing threat of the climate crisis to our existence. This involves slowing them down and encouraging their awareness of and engagement with what is around them. I draw on Australian and New Zealand Indigenous relationships with nature but also on the Japanese art of *shinrin yoku*. This means relaxing in nature such as in a forest or grove/stand of trees, feeling it and allowing it to make your mind and body healthy. Research supports its health benefits.

Our family Airbnb business is more than just a business. It gives us great joy because of how our guests pick up on the love Chiho and I put into it and the amazing natural environment they find themselves in. We believe that good energy can attract people with similar energy, and our guests confirm this. Of course, the money matters, but the pleasure we get from knowing how much our guests enjoy their stays is equally as important for us.

We also hope that the connection with nature many guests feel can make a small contribution to improving their awareness of nature. They may not quite harmonise with nature but certainly for some, this will be a chance to get closer to it and feel a little of the peace and relaxation it can engender. As Greg suggested, when having his Indigenous students plant trees at the Pulardi school in the Tanami Desert, we should all do our little bit for the natural environment. That was over thirty years ago, but it is even more relevant today. We do our little bit by planting some trees beyond the creek for koalas and other wildlife like sugar gliders and birds.

Some guests' experiences can be engaging enough for Chiho to think that, anyone who stayed in the Villa for a week might have to readjust when they get home. She may be right, and this is what happened to me from the age of fourteen. My experiences of growing up in Byron Bay kick-started a life journey shaped by dealing with grief and growing through the experience. The deaths in my family provided the challenges needed for me to learn, reflect, know myself, grow, and make me who I am today. My core beliefs, values, and dispositions were developed early in my life and shaped by my family and home. Subsequent development came from experience, living in and adapting to different environments, taking on challenges, learning how to go with the flow, and being able to trust my spirit.

Dealing with these deaths, and particularly the shocking ways in which Greg and Sue died could have destroyed me. Instead, it made a big contribution toward me becoming the person I am now through a long process of self-discovery. Like anyone else, I have my faults and weaknesses that I am still working on, but learning to deal with grief made a huge contribution to where I am now on my life journey.

One Sunday morning after coffee at Crystalbrook (formerly Byron at Byron), Chiho and I went for a walk with two good friends through the Tea-tree swamp on the chunky natural timber boardwalk. Taking in the beautiful environment around us, Chiho and I read several Buddhist proverbs that had deep meaning for us both. We also read an Australian Aboriginal proverb that I use here to finish this book because it captures my approach to life that has been shaped by dealing with grief and is rooted in the influence of my family and home.

> We are all visitors to this time, this place. We are just passing through. Our purpose here is to observe, to learn, to grow, to love… and then we must return home.

Further reading

Csikszentmihalyi, M. (1997). *Finding flow: The psychology of engagement with everyday life*. New York: Basic Books.

Dewey, J. (1938) *Experience and Education*. New York: Kappa Delta.

Dowrick, S. (2021, July 17-18). Wisdom walks in two worlds. *The Sydney Morning Herald, Spectrum*, p. 9.

Gillian, K. (2022, May 1) Still riding the wave, *The Sun Herald*, pp. 32-33.

Grogan, J. (2013). *Encountering America: Humanistic psychology, sixties culture and the shaping of the modern self*, New York, London, Toronto, Sydney, New Delhi & Auckland: Harper Perennial.

Hawley, J. (2023, April 15). Olsen's final chapter. *Sydney Morning Herald*, pp. 28-29.

Edited version of chapter in *Artists in Conversation* by Janet Hawley, Slattery Media.

Leventhal, D. H. (2023). *Make it meaningful: Finding purpose in life and work*. London, New York, Sydney & New Delhi: Simon & Schuster

Miriam-Rose Ungunmerr-Baumann, Dadirri. Available at: http://www.yarrahealing.catholic.edu.au/celebrations/index.cfm?loadref=58

Mitchell, Thomas (2022, April 27) The toiling toddlers teaching life lessons, *The Sydney Morning Herald*, p. 3.